Numerology

Made Easy

❖ Also in the Made Easy series ❖

The Akashic Records
Animal Communication
Astrology
Chakras
Connecting with the Angels
Connecting with the Fairies
Crystals
Discovering Your Past Lives
Energy Healing
Feng Shui
Goddess Wisdom
Lucid Dreaming
Meditation
Mediumship
Mindfulness
NLP
Qabalah
Reiki
Self-Hypnosis
Shamanism
Tantra
Tarot

Numerology

Made Easy

Discover Your Future,
Life Purpose and Destiny
from Your Birth Date
and Name

Michelle Buchanan

HAY HOUSE
Carlsbad, California • New York City
London • Sydney • New Delhi

Published in the United Kingdom by:
Hay House UK, Ltd., The Sixth Floor, Watson House,
54 Baker Street, London W1U 7BU
Phone: +44 (0)20 3927 7290 • Fax: +44 (0)20 3927 7291
www.hayhouse.co.uk

Published in the United States of America by:
Hay House LLC, PO Box 5100, Carlsbad, CA 92018-5100
Tel: (1) 760 431 7695 or (800) 654 5126
Fax: (1) 760 431 6948 or (800) 650 5115; www.hayhouse.com

Published in Australia by:
Hay House Australia Ltd, 18/36 Ralph St, Alexandria NSW 2015
Tel: (61) 2 9669 4299; Fax: (61) 2 9669 4144; www.hayhouse.com.au

Published in India by:
Hay House Publishers India, Muskaan Complex, Plot No.3, B-2,
Vasant Kunj, New Delhi 110 070
Tel: (91) 11 4176 1620; Fax: (91) 11 4176 1630; www.hayhouse.co.in

This book was previously published as *Numerology* (*Hay House Basics* series); ISBN: 978-1-78180-556-5

A catalogue record for this book is available from the British Library.

17 16 15 14 13 12 11 10 9 8

ISBN: 978-1-78817-258-5

Printed in the United States of America

Contents

Introduction

How I discovered numerology

Ever since I was a little girl, I dreamed of being a singer. I sang Elvis songs with my dad at the age of five; I performed Blondie songs in front of my school at the age of nine; I wrote original songs and was the lead singer for various rock bands throughout my teens; and I worked for a major record company when I was 19. Music was my life and there wasn't a doubt in my mind that I would become an international rock star when I left New Zealand for Los Angeles in 1991 – all bright-eyed and bushy-tailed at the age of 21.

As soon as I hit the LA music scene, things took a different turn. When I discovered the high standard of competition and the fact that thousands of other talented hopefuls were scrambling for the very same dream, my confidence took a dive and my ambition went out the window. Back then I believed the other girls had more talent and were ten times better-looking than me. I felt there was no way I could possibly compete – and I didn't even want to try. What made the situation worse was that never in my life had I ever even *contemplated* plan B!

There I was, all alone, on the other side of the world, with no hope of living my dream. The realization hit me hard and before long I was on a downward spiral fueled by bulimia and drugs. Over the months that followed, I lost my dream, my identity, and my self-esteem. I was lost, unsure of my life purpose, and I had no hope at all for my future. During this time a friend told me about a numerologist who gave personal readings from her home in Venice Beach. Knowing I wouldn't book a reading of my own accord, she gifted me a 40-minute session to ensure I would definitely attend.

Even though I believed in the spirit world and was drawn to metaphysics as a child, I didn't know a thing about numerology. My mother was a fan of astrology and at the age of 12, I would take her Linda Goodman books to school to read star-sign descriptions for my friends. I didn't have a clue how numerology worked, but like a typical "know-it-all Aries," I assumed it was a load of rubbish and didn't give it the time of day. Heading into my reading, I had no expectation of the outcome and thought it would be a complete waste of time.

To this day, I'm still ashamed of my ignorance and closed-mindedness for judging numerology in such a negative way, because that 40-minute reading was phenomenal and it literally changed my life! They say, "There's no such thing as a coincidence" and "When the student is ready, the teacher will appear" – I can confirm from personal experience that this was definitely the case for me. Not only was my reading extraordinary, accurate, and empowering, but it also introduced me to my potential and inspired me to want to achieve it.

In my reading, the numerologist revealed another side of me that I'd seen glimpses of, but hadn't fully explored. She emphasized my capabilities and taught me to see myself (and my life) from a deeper and broader perspective. Because she discussed my personality traits and challenges at the *beginning* of the reading, I was able to see how accurate numerology really was. She didn't know me from a bar of soap, so it provided the credibility I needed to take on board everything else she had to say.

When she spoke of my weaknesses and typical life challenges, it helped me to see that I wasn't the type of person I was or in the predicament I was in because I was a hopeless loser. I was the type of person I was and in the predicament I was in because it was typical of my "numbers." As strange as it sounds, I found reassurance and an overwhelming sense of peace in that discovery. Knowing that it was "normal" to face the challenges I faced enabled me to begin the long and progressive journey toward self-love and understanding – a journey that might not have begun at all if I hadn't discovered my "numbers".

Now, 24 years later, I'm an international numerologist and author of two numerology books as well as the world's first deck of numerology oracle cards, giving personal readings and teaching numerology to people all over the world. After 24 years of independent study, I'm living my dream of helping others through the undeniable power of numbers. This makes my life worth living – and thousands of readings later, the accuracy of numerology continues to amaze me.

Knowing what I now know about manifestation, there are times when I wish I'd kept pursuing my dream of being a singer by applying the principles of the Law of Attraction. I have the same 38/11/2 Life Path Number as Madonna and the same March 28 birthday as Lady Gaga – so maybe I could've made it if I'd kept trying instead of running away at the first sign of competition? That said, I strongly believe the Universe (God/Divine/Source) knows what it's doing and it had other plans for me. Although I still sing as a hobby, nothing makes me happier than assisting others on their path with the gift of numerology. I'm so grateful to have discovered this precious, life-changing tool, and I wouldn't change it for a thing – not even an international singing career and 20 number-one singles! And that's the honest truth.

How numerology improved my life

Numerology has improved my life in many ways. First of all, it enabled me to see myself in a direct, honest, and non-biased way – which helps when you're on a journey of personal transformation. It showed me how to view my life from a deeper and broader perspective, and to see it as a blueprint. This helped me to "de-personalize" my challenges and see them as opportunities for growth, which are necessary for the evolution of my soul.

Numerology has taught me that regardless of how difficult my challenges may be, I was born with the ability to overcome them – which is one of the reasons I chose them in the first place. That information really helps when you're trying to make sense of your problems and are searching for a light at the end of the tunnel. More than anything, numerology has helped me understand, accept, and make peace with myself. This has been one of my greatest achievements to date, because I hated myself for years.

Thanks to numerology, I was able to recognize (and take responsibility for) my shortcomings so I could begin improving myself and creating a better life. Knowing my destiny, life purpose, and future potential has inspired me to become a better person and to make the most of my life – and for that I'm truly grateful. Here are some of the reasons why numerology has improved my life.

Numerology has:

- Reassured me that I'm on the right path
- Uncovered my pre-chosen destiny
- Confirmed my life purpose
- Revealed my future potential
- Provided a tool to better understand others
- Shown me other possibilities for my life
- Helped me to prepare for upcoming challenges
- Given me direction in life
- Enabled me to take advantage of opportunities coming my way
- Provided my life's blueprint
- Made me aware of my strengths and weaknesses
- Helped me to forecast and plan my future
- Improved my relationships with others

And one more thing... numerology even helped me to make the biggest dream of my life come true. That's right! Understanding my numerology blueprint helped me to get my book *The Numerology Guidebook* and oracle cards *Numerology Guidance Cards* published by Hay House, so I could share numerology with the world.

Now, my wish for you is that numerology will help to make your dreams come true, too.

What is numerology?

Everything in the universe has an energy vibration – and numbers are no different. In fact, every number (and letter) has its own unique vibration that contributes an influence upon the story of your life. Therefore, numerology is the study of the relationship that numbers and letters have with our personality and life events. It is an ancient metaphysical science that reveals the blueprint of every human being's life and it is one of the most accurate and powerful self-help tools available today.

From a spiritual perspective, you have a soul within your physical body that has chosen to incarnate into this life simply to evolve through the life experiences it encounters while it's here. Throughout the course of this life there are specific areas of growth your soul has chosen to master and specific opportunities it would like to take advantage of on its journey. In order to do this there are specific personality traits and life circumstances it requires in order to achieve its goal – the details of which are found in your "numbers." In other words, your numerology profile uncovers the blueprint of what your soul has pre-chosen to accomplish in this life.

One of the benefits of numerology is that it can uncover your destiny and life purpose and the life lessons you'll face along the way, which is valuable information if you want to make the most of your journey. Numerology is so much more than predicting the future, or choosing the ideal partner, date, or name. It's the bridge between who you are now and who you have the potential to be. It's a stepping-stone that enables you to live your best life and be the best that you can be.

Where did numerology originate?

There are several systems of numerology originating from various civilizations, time periods, and locations across the world. It is said that it originally dates back thousands of years to the ancient civilizations of Atlantis, Babylon, China, Egypt, India, and Greece. The Chaldean system of numerology (developed by the Chaldeans of ancient Babylon) is believed to be the oldest system of all; however, modern numerologists believe it is outdated and isn't very accurate today.

Western (otherwise known as "modern" numerology) is by far the most popular and accurate system used around the world today. Western numerology was created by the Greek philosopher and mathematician, Pythagoras, more than 2,500 years ago. Pythagoras is considered to be the father of modern numerology and the person who put numerology on the map. Other numerology systems currently being used worldwide include the Kabbalistic, Chinese, and Tamil/Indian.

Interesting fact

The mathematician Pythagoras created the "Pythagorean theorem" – one of the most famous theorems in mathematics. It describes the relationship between the three sides of a right triangle and is still taught in secondary-school mathematics classes around the world today. Pythagoras certainly knew his stuff and when it comes to the credibility of numerology and where it stems from, I like to ask: If Pythagoras was considered a genius of the ages, why would he create something that was complete load of rubbish? I rest my case.

What can numerology be used for?

Numerology can be used for many things, but here are some of its most common uses:

- Greater awareness and self-understanding
- Improving relationships through a better understanding of others
- Forecasting the future
- Planning major life events
- Predicting cycles and patterns
- Choosing a suitable career
- Evaluating relationship compatibility
- Changing a name for marriage (or other purposes)
- Choosing a business name (product name, brand name, book title etc ...)
- Naming a baby

- Evaluating the energy of an address, a property, or a home
- Choosing a wedding date
- Naming a pet
- Deciphering the meaning of recurring numbers
- Evaluating the energy of a country, a city, a town etc.

The benefits of numerology

The greatest benefit of numerology is the gift of insight. To be forewarned is to be forearmed, and numerology provides the road map for your life so you have an idea of where you're going and what to expect along the way. If you decided to take a road trip to an unfamiliar destination, wouldn't you prefer to consult a map to see where you're going and check the driving conditions before you hit the road? Numerology is a tool that can help you to find your destination and to arrive there safely, too.

In addition, numerology uncovers your potential and shows you what you have the ability to achieve. It helps with goal-setting and planning your future and it gives you reassurance that you're on the right path. Another advantage is that it enables you to prepare for potential challenges and to grasp the opportunities coming your way.

How numerology can improve your life

Numerology gives your life meaning. It takes it from being a "random event" to a pre-planned blueprint of opportunity and potential. It offers direction and added insight into what's around the corner, and it uncovers your destiny and life purpose. It also provides a deeper understanding of others and the world around you. How can than *not* improve your life?

How to use numerology

Along with any form of prediction or divination, numerology is best used as a guide to complement your life. Combined with intuition, sound decision-making, and plain old common sense, it should be used as a tool to help you to navigate your life better.

Just in case you were wondering ... numerology can't predict winning lottery numbers or a person's time of death. (But it might be handy if it could).

Interesting fact

You don't have to be good at mathematics to learn numerology – the equations are simple and only require basic addition and subtraction. All you need is a calculator, some paper, and a pen. On second thoughts, you'd better make that a pencil with an eraser, just in case.

How to read a chart

The key to reading a numerology chart and obtaining an accurate summary of your life is to "blend everything together." There are many pieces of the numerology puzzle and your numerology chart is a matrix of interconnecting numbers and influences that can only be accurately interpreted with dedication, patience, and time.

The best way to read a chart is to break it into segments starting with the Personality Numbers. Take your time getting to know each number and its position, then blend them all together using your intuition and common sense to interpret what that could mean.

When you're ready, bring in the short-term Forecasting Numbers such as the Personal Year and the Personal Month Numbers to get an idea of how these numbers are currently influencing your life on an everyday basis. Once you have a handle on those, introduce the long-term Forecasting Numbers, such as the Pinnacles, Challenges, and Major Life Cycles, to determine the overriding influences affecting your life long term. This book has been laid out in this particular order to help you do just that.

Rome wasn't built in a day and you're not expected to understand a complete numerology chart overnight. Professional numerologists take years to perfect their art and there is always more to learn. Don't set your expectations too high. Instead, pace yourself and take your time. The less pressure you put upon yourself in the beginning, the easier it will be to interpret the numbers.

Interesting fact

When it comes to the Forecasting Numbers, *a number has the same meaning wherever it appears*, so once you have an understanding of each number and what it represents, you can interpret its influence wherever it appears.

How to use this book

This book is laid out in the simplest way possible to help you learn numerology with ease. To make your learning experience as useful as possible, the book is divided into three main categories: The Personality Numbers (*see page 1*), The Forecasting Numbers (*see page 111*), and Other Numbers Around You (*see page 209*).

In the Personality Numbers section you'll discover the seven Personality Numbers that make up a personality profile. These numbers will reveal your strengths, weaknesses, and typical personality traits, as well as your destiny, life purpose, and future potential. You'll learn the easiest way to calculate these numbers so you can create a detailed personality profile for others and yourself.

Once you've calculated a personality profile from the seven Personality Numbers, you can begin to uncover their meanings in the Personality Number Meanings section (*see page 29*), which will reveal the top five strengths, the top five challenges, and suitable career choices for each number. It will also provide a case study of a real person's experience of living with that number, which will enable you to see how the number expresses itself in their life.

Following that is a Meditation for each number. This will enable you to adopt, enhance, and integrate the positive personality traits of each number into your own life, whether you have that number in your personality profile or not.

Next, we move on to the short-term Forecasting Numbers to help you predict your short-term future. That way you can prepare for (and take advantage of) what's coming your way in the approaching days, months, and years.

Here we begin with the Personal Year Number that includes:

- a forecast for the year – what you can expect for the year
- "A year to..." – a recommended plan of action for the year
- Michelle's manifestation tip – manifestation tips to help you manifest your goals and dreams
- an affirmation – a positive affirmation for the year

Then, we move on to the Personal Month Number to give you an idea of what's expected for the month. Following that, I've included a Personal Year and Personal Month Combination Forecast for each of the 12 months within each year. This will help you to forecast your year and month combinations with greater accuracy and ease.

Following the Personal Year and Personal Month Numbers, we take a look at the Personal Day Numbers. This will give you an idea of the energy around you on a daily basis, so you can better plan your day. In order for you to recognize the broader dynamics that affect your everyday life, we'll take a look at the Universal Year, Universal Month, and Universal Day Numbers – and add those into the mix as well.

Next, we move on to the long-term Forecasting Numbers to help you predict your future further ahead. That way you can prepare for (and take advantage of) what's coming your way in the current and distant years. Here we discuss the Pinnacles, Challenges, and Major Life Cycles that provide your important opportunities, obstacles, and experiences.

The final section of the book focuses on some of the other numbers around you in your everyday life, such as recurring numbers like 11:11. Here you can learn what these numbers (and other number sequences) mean and what the Universe is trying to tell you. If you're curious about the energy within and around your home, this is where you would come to explore House Numbers. Perhaps you're looking for a website or a business name - or maybe a brand name, a book title, or a product name - or any other name for that matter! Other Numbers Around You will cover that as well.

As you navigate your way through the book you'll find many Interesting fact boxes that provide handy titbits of information to make learning numerology easier.

And if you're forgetful or are easily confused, you'll find a helpful Glossary at the back to remind you of the numerology terms and what they mean.

In the Recommended Reading section at the back of the book, I'll introduce you to some of my favourite numerology books of all time. Should you wish to develop your knowledge of numerology further, there's also a Further Resources section, which will point you in the right direction.

By the time you finish this book, you'll see that your life purpose has nothing to do with how much money you have, what you do for a living, or what you have or haven't accomplished. Instead it has to do with the person you are and how you see the world. This book will show you that you're exactly as you're meant to be and you're already on the right path! So grab some paper, and a pen or a pencil with an eraser, and a calculator for greater accuracy ... and prepare to uncover your destiny and the blueprint of your life.

Interesting fact

- It isn't necessary to know your time or location of birth in numerology – this is only needed for astrology. Numerology involves the study of letters and numbers, while astrology focuses on the planets and the stars.

Before we start calculating the numbers, let me tell you about a major Numerology Rule of Thumb you're going to come across while learning numerology.

Numerology rule of thumb

In numerology, a common rule of thumb you're going to encounter is: *continue adding numbers together until you get a single digit number between 1 and 9.*

For example: 3421 would be 3+4+2+1 = 10

1+0 = 1

The only time this rule doesn't apply is when you come across a number 11, 22, or 33. When this happens you don't add the 1 and 1, the 2 and 2, or the 3 and 3 together – instead, the 11 becomes an 11/2, the 22 becomes a 22/4, and the 33 becomes a 33/6. We'll talk more about this later (*see page 89*).

For now, let's start by taking a look at the Personality Numbers.

Part I

THE PERSONALITY NUMBERS

Within your numerology chart, these seven numbers are the most significant in determining your personality and life's journey.

Introduction

The personality profile

In numerology, a personality profile consists of seven Personality Numbers that make a person who they are. The key to an accurate reading lies in your ability to "blend" each of those seven numbers together.

I like to think of a personality profile as a seven-piece puzzle. Each of the seven pieces plays its own unique part, but it's the combination of all seven pieces together that makes the puzzle complete. If a piece of the numerology puzzle is missing, a person's story is incomplete, so you need each of the seven pieces to create an accurate summary of your personality and life.

Blending all of the numbers together takes practice, patience, and time. However, once you get the hang of it, you'll be reading a numerology chart like a pro.

The seven Personality Numbers are:

- the Life Path Number
- the Destiny Number

- the Soul Number
- the Personality Number
- the Maturity Number
- the Current Name Number
- the Birth Day Number

These numbers are calculated from the full, original birth-certificate name, the date of birth, and the current first and last names used today.

Interesting fact

Sometimes the Personality Numbers can have different names. For example, the Destiny Number may be called the Expression Number and the Life Path Number may be called the Ruling Number. I'll inform you of these things as we go along, so nothing surprises you in the future.

Now let's get started with the first, and most important, of the seven Personality Numbers – the Life Path Number.

The Life Path Number

Of the seven Personality Numbers, your Life Path Number is the most significant of all. It provides the most information about your character and the type of life you'll live.

Your Life Path Number uncovers your life purpose and the path you've chosen to walk in this life. It indicates the kind of life experiences you'll encounter and the lessons you'll learn along the way.

The Life Path Number is also known as the Ruling Number, the Birth Number, the Birth Path, or the Birth Force Number. In Chaldean numerology it is called the Destiny Number.

How to calculate the Life Path Number

Your Life Path Number is calculated by adding all of the numbers in your birth date together. There are three ways to do this; however the two most commonly used methods are "adding across" and "reducing down." Neither method is right or wrong – they're just different. The method used is simply a matter of personal preference.

Adding across

This is how to calculate a Life Path Number by adding across:

Step 1: Add together all of the numbers in your birth date by adding them across.

Make sure you write the full birth year – for example, 1969 rather than just 69.

Let's use the birth date October 11, 1969 (10–11–1969), as an example:

1+0+1+1+1+9+6+9 = 28

Step 2: Continue adding any double-digit numbers together until you get a single-digit Life Path Number between 1 and 9 unless it totals 11, 22, or 33, which then becomes an 11/2, 22/4, or 33/6.

2+8 = 10

1+0 = **1 Life Path Number**

Now, let's see what happens when we get a total of 33, as with birth date January 8, 1968 (1-8-1968)

1+8+1+9+6+8 = **33 Life Path Number**

Since we do not add 11, 22, or 33 together, this would be a 33/6 Life Path Number.

Interesting fact

Most professional numerologists do not recognize 33/6 as a Master Number when it is calculated using the adding-across method, so they will reduce it down to a 6. They only recognize a 33/6 Master Number when it is calculated using the reducing-down method.

(We'll discuss Master Numbers a little later on (*see page 89*).)

Reducing down

Let's take a look at the reducing-down method now. This is how to calculate a Life Path Number by reducing down:

Step 1: Reduce the month, day, and year numbers of your birth date down to three single-digit numbers unless they total 11 or 22. (If they total 11 or 22, don't reduce them down - keep them as 11 or 22).

Let's use the birth date December 11, 1969 (12–11–1969), as an example:

1+2 / 11 / 1+9+6+9 = 25

3 **11** 2+5

7

Step 2: Add the single totals together (and 11 and 22, where applicable) and continue adding any double-digit numbers together until you get a single-digit Life Path Number between 1 and 9. If a Life Path Number totals 11, 22, or 33, it doesn't reduce down to 2, 4, or 6. It remains 11, 22, or 33 and becomes an 11/2, 22/4, or 33/6 Life Path Number.

3+11+7 = 21

2+1 = **3 Life Path Number**

Now let's see what happens with the birth date January 8, 1968 (1-8-1968) that previously gave us a 33/6 Life Path Number using the adding-across method (*see page 6*).

1 / 8 / 1+9+6+8 = 24

1 8 2+4

6

1+8+6 = 15

1+5 = **6 Life Path Number**

As you can see, the reducing-down method gave us 15 (prior to a reducing-down to a 6 Life Path Number) and the adding-across method gave us 33. So how do we know which method is correct? One of the most confusing things about numerology is that we don't. All I can say is that most professional numerologists believe the reducing-down method is the most accurate of all when determining a genuine Master Number of 11/2, 22/4, or 33/6. (We'll discuss this in further detail a little later on – *see page 89*).

Interesting fact

If you end up with an 11/2, 22/4, or 33/6 by adding across, you can determine which is the most accurate fit for you by reading the number descriptions for both the 11/2, 22/4, or 33/6 and the regular 2, 4, or 6 in the Personality Number Meanings section that follows (*see page 29*).

Next, let me introduce the Destiny Number.

The Destiny Number

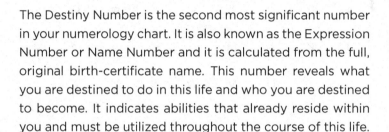

The Destiny Number is the second most significant number in your numerology chart. It is also known as the Expression Number or Name Number and it is calculated from the full, original birth-certificate name. This number reveals what you are destined to do in this life and who you are destined to become. It indicates abilities that already reside within you and must be utilized throughout the course of this life. Along with the Life Path Number, this is the number to take into consideration when choosing a career.

The full, original birth-certificate name is required to calculate the Destiny Number regardless of whether you still use that name or not – and regardless of whether you were adopted or have since changed your name through marriage or other means. Even if you only had that birth certificate name for one day, and even if that birth-certificate name was simply "Baby," this is the name that must be used.

Interesting fact

The original birth-certificate name uncovers your pre-chosen destiny that remains with you forever. The energy of this name (and its accompanying Destiny Number) doesn't disappear when you change your name. It is always a major influence throughout the course of your life.

How to calculate the Destiny Number

1	2	3	4	5	6	7	8	9
A	B	C	D	E	F	G	H	I
J	K	L	M	N	O	P	Q	R
S	T	U	V	W	X	Y	Z	

Step 1: Using the Western Pythagorean letters-and-numbers chart above, write your full, original birth-certificate name and match the corresponding numbers to each letter.

Please note a hyphenated or compound last name is considered one name and titles such as Junior (Jr.) and Senior (Sr.) are not included in the calculation. If you don't have a middle name, you only need to calculate your first and last name. If you have several middle names, you need to calculate each middle name separately.

Be sure to leave plenty of space between each letter so you don't leave out a number by mistake.

Interesting fact

It pays to double-check the spelling on your birth certificate to ensure that everything is correct. You'd be surprised how many people forget to include their middle name or have unknowingly spelled their birth-certificate name incorrectly their whole lives.

Let's use the name Mary Ann Smith as an example:

MARY	ANN	SMITH
4+1+9+7	1+5+5	1+4+9+2+8

Step 2: Add each name separately to create individual totals.

MARY	ANN	SMITH
4+1+9+7	1+5+5	1+4+9+2+8
21	11	24

Step 3: Add double-digit totals together to create single-number totals unless they total 11, 22, or 33. (If they total 11, 22, or 33 don't reduce them down - keep them as 11, 22 or 33).

MARY	ANN	SMITH
4+1+9+7	1+5+5	1+4+9+2+8
21	11	24
2+1	11	2+4
3	**11**	**6**

Step 4: Add the single totals together (and 11, 22, and 33 where applicable) and continue adding any double-digit

numbers together until you get a single-digit Destiny Number between 1 and 9. If a Destiny Number totals 11, 22, or 33, it doesn't reduce down to 2, 4, or 6. It remains 11, 22, or 33 and becomes an 11/2, 22/4, or 33/6 Destiny Number.

3+11+6 = 20

2+0 = **2 Destiny Number**

You're going to use this exact same process to calculate your Current Name Number, Business Name Number, and any other name numbers for that matter - so I suggest you bookmark this page for future reference. Also, keep these calculations handy, as you'll need to refer back to them to calculate your Karmic Lesson Numbers a little further on (*see page 24*).

Next, let's move on to the Soul Number.

The Soul Number

The Soul Number is the third most significant number in your numerology chart and it is also known as the Soul's Urge, Soul's Desire, or Heart's Desire. It reveals what your soul needs (and desires) you to be, in order to feel complete. In other words, if you were to adopt the positive traits of this number, your soul would feel content and complete.

The Soul Number is calculated from the *vowels* in your birth-certificate name.

Interesting fact

Y is sometimes a consonant, and other times it's a vowel. Y is considered a vowel when there are no other vowels in the syllable or when the Y is next to (or in between) two consonants, such as in the names Wynn, Yvette, and Mary.

How to calculate the Soul Number

Step 1: Add up the numbers that correspond to the vowels in your birth-certificate name.

Step 2: Add each name separately to create individual totals. Add double-digit totals together to create single-number totals (unless they total 11, 22 or 33 which remain 11, 22, or 33).

MARY	ANN	SMITH
1 7	**1**	**9**
1 + 7	1	9
8		

Step 3: Add the single totals together (and 11, 22, and 33 where applicable) and continue adding any double-digit numbers together until you get a single-digit Soul Number between 1 and 9. If a Soul Number totals 11, 22, or 33, it doesn't reduce down to 2, 4, or 6. It remains 11, 22, or 33 and becomes an 11/2, 22/4, or 33/6 Soul Number.

8+1+9 = 18

1+8 = **9 Soul Number**

Now, let's take a look at the Personality Number.

The Personality Number

The Personality Number is the least significant of the seven Personality Numbers. It is also known as the Outer You or the Outer Personality Number because it gives an indication as to how others perceive you and is said to represent the "outer you." It is calculated from the consonants in your birth-certificate name.

Interesting fact

The personality traits of the more dominant numbers in your chart such as the Life Path, Destiny, Soul, and Birth Day Numbers (as well as your astrology Sun Sign) tend to overshadow the Personality Number – therefore this number may not provide an accurate evaluation of one's personality and how it is perceived by others.

How to calculate the Personality Number

Step 1: Add the numbers in your birth-certificate name that are consonants.

Step 2: Add each name separately to create individual totals. Add double-digit totals together to create single-number totals (unless they total 11, 22 or 33 which remain 11, 22, or 33).

MARY	ANN	SMITH
4 + 9	5+5	1+4 + 2+8
13	10	15
1+3	1+0	1+5
4	1	6

Step 3: Add the single totals together (and 11, 22, and 33 where applicable) and continue adding any double-digit numbers together until you get a single-digit Personality Number between 1 and 9. If a Personality Number totals 11, 22, or 33, it doesn't reduce down to 2, 4, or 6. It remains 11, 22, or 33 and becomes an 11/2, 22/4, or 33/6 Personality Number.

4+1+6 = 11/2 Personality Number

Interesting fact

A great way to double-check your answers is to remember this handy little equation:

The Soul Number (vowels) + the Personality Number (consonants) = the Destiny Number (total name)

The Maturity Number

The Maturity Number is a very significant number in your chart because it reveals your future potential and the ultimate goal of your life. It tells you where your destiny is leading you and what you can expect from the second half of your life. It is also known at the Power Number, Attainment Number, or Realization Number. It is the number to keep in mind when making long-term goals and decisions.

Interesting fact

The Maturity Number doesn't kick in until maturity or midlife, from the age of 45 onwards. This is an accumulative energy and as each year passes the influence of your Maturity Number strengthens and matures. By the age of 50, you should feel its influence in your life.

How to calculate the Maturity Number

The Maturity Number is calculated by adding the Life Path Number and Destiny Number together.

Step 1: Add your Life Path Number and Destiny Number together.

Step 2: Add any double-digit totals together to create a single-digit Maturity Number unless they total 11, 22, or 33, which then becomes an 11/2, 22/4, or 33/6 Maturity Number.

Let's use Mary Ann Smith's 3 Life Path Number and 11/2 Destiny Number as an example.

3 Life Path Number + 11/2 Destiny Number = 14

1+4 = 5 Maturity Number

Now let's move on to the Current Name Number.

The Current Name Number

The Current Name Number is the "first" and "last" name you currently use on a daily basis today. It is also known as the Minor Expression Number and for some people it's a shortened version of the birth certificate name. For others it's a new name altogether due to marriage, adoption, or some other reason.

The Current Name Number is an indication of the vibration you're projecting out into the world every time you use that name. It is your "energetic signature" that brings additional personality traits, strengths, lessons, experiences, and opportunities to your existing profile of numbers.

Interesting fact

If you're thinking of changing your name for marriage (or any other reason), you definitely want to calculate your new Current Name Number to get an indication of how that name will affect your personality and life. You may find you prefer the Current Name Number you already have and decide not to change your name after all. This happens a lot.

How to calculate the Current Name Number

The Current Name Number is calculated using the exact same method used to calculate the Destiny Number. Please note, a hyphenated or compound last name is considered one name.

Let's use Mary Ann Smith's current and married name, Mary Jones, as an example:

MARY	JONES
4+1+9+7	1+6+5+5+1
21	18
2+1 = 3	1+8 = 9

3+9 = 12

1+2 = 3 Current Name Number

Last, but certainly by no means least – let's take a look at the Birth Day Number.

The Birth Day Number

The Birth Day Number is simply the "day" of the month you were born on and it is otherwise known as the Day Number or the Day Born Number. It reveals additional personality traits along with specific talents and abilities that will assist you on your life path.

How to calculate the Birth Day Number

Reduce the day of the month you were born to a single-digit number.

If you were born on a single-digit day, that is your Birth Day Number, and if you were born on a double-digit day, add the numbers together to get a single-digit Birth Day Number.

If you were born on the 11th or 29th, it would become an 11/2 Birth Day Number, and a birthday on the 22nd is a 22/4 Birth Day Number.

For example:

June 8, 1972 = **8 Birth Day Number**

April 23, 1983 = 2+3 = **5 Birth Day Number**

December 29, 2001 = 2+9 = **11/2 Birth Day Number**

May 22, 1954 = **22/4 Birth Day Number**

Now that you've calculated the seven Personality Numbers, let's have a chat about karma. Starting with the Karmic Lesson Numbers – another significant aspect of your numerology chart.

Karmic Numbers

Karmic Lesson Numbers

Karmic Lesson Numbers indicate some of your inherited weaknesses and specific areas in need of growth that have been passed on from your previous lives and need to be addressed in this life. One of the reasons you've chosen to incarnate into this current life is to learn to master them once and for all. If you have a Karmic Lesson Number in your numerology chart, that karmic lesson will continually present itself throughout your life until you've worked it out.

Some people have several Karmic Lesson Numbers, and some have none. However, if you're fortunate enough not to have any, it doesn't mean you're going to have an easy, trouble-free life. It simply means that the majority of your challenges will come through the other numbers in your chart.

Interesting fact

The influence of a Karmic Lesson Number is minimized when that number is your Life Path, Destiny, Soul, Personality, Maturity, or Birth Day Number. For example, if you have a Karmic Lesson Number 8 and you're an 8 Life Path, the karmic lesson is reduced.

So, let's start working out your Karmic Lesson Numbers by referring back to your Destiny Number calculations based on your original birth-certificate name.

How to calculate the Karmic Lesson Numbers

Karmic Lesson Numbers are calculated from the missing numbers between 1 and 9 in a birth-certificate name, indicating karmic lessons.

If every number between 1 and 9 is present, then you have no karmic lessons; however, any number that is missing is a Karmic Lesson Number. Let's take a look at Mary Ann Smith's name to see if she has any Karmic Lesson Numbers.

M A R Y A N N S M I T H
4 1 9 7 1 5 5 1 4 9 2 8

As you can see, Mary is missing numbers 3 and 6 from her name; therefore, she has a 3 Karmic Lesson Number and a 6 Karmic Lesson Number.

Because Mary has a 3 Life Path Number and 3 Current Name Number, the influence of her 3 Karmic Lesson Number is minimized. However, because she doesn't have a number 6 among her Personality Numbers, she'll need to overcome her 6 Karmic Lesson Number in this lifetime.

Interesting fact

Karmic Lesson Numbers are also known as Missing Numbers because they indicate the numbers that are 'missing' in your birth-certificate name.

Karmic Lesson Number meanings

Karmic Lesson Number 1: This lesson indicates a need to be more courageous, independent, and self-sufficient in this life. This lesson will force you to stand up for yourself, to embrace your individuality, and to walk a path less traveled.

Karmic Lesson Number 2: This lesson indicates a need to be more cooperative, patient, and considerate toward others. This lesson will force you to be more aware of others' feelings, to harmonize with your environment, and to learn to work as part of a team.

Karmic Lesson Number 3: This lesson indicates a need to be more confident and appreciative of your talents. This lesson will force you to lighten up and to be more joyful and easy-going. It will also force you to be less critical of yourself and life.

Karmic Lesson Number 4: This lesson indicates a need to be more organized, disciplined, and focused. This lesson will make you take your commitments seriously and work hard to achieve your goals. It will also force you to be responsible and reliable.

Karmic Lesson Number 5: This lesson indicates a need to be more open, adaptable, and welcoming of change. This lesson will force you to take advantage of the opportunities and experiences you are given and to be more outgoing and adventurous in life.

Karmic Lesson Number 6: This lesson indicates a need to be more responsible, dedicated, and committed to others and life. This lesson will force you to take your responsibilities seriously and to establish genuine and meaningful relationships with others.

Karmic Lesson Number 7: This lesson indicates a need to look beyond the physical world to discover the deeper meaning of life. This lesson will force you to be more trusting of others and yourself. It will encourage you to be open-minded and to find a spiritual faith.

Karmic Lesson Number 8: This lesson indicates a need to reclaim your personal power over whatever disempowers you. This lesson will force you to understand money, status, authority, and power. It will encourage you to learn how to manage your material affairs.

Karmic Lesson Number 9: This lesson indicates a need to be more understanding, tolerant, and less judgmental of others. This lesson will force you to learn forgiveness and to broaden your understanding of others and life.

Karmic Debt Numbers

While we're on the subject of karma, let's discuss Karmic Debt Numbers.

If you have a 13/4, 14/5, 16/7, or 19/1 in your seven Personality Numbers, it's considered a Karmic Debt Number. Karmic Debt Numbers indicate particular lessons that must be mastered in *this* lifetime because we failed to learn them in previous lives. Each Karmic Debt Number has its own unique lessons and burdens. Let's see what they are:

Karmic Debt Number 13/4: This number indicates that extra effort is required to master discipline, integrity, and determination in this life. With a 13/4 among your Personality Numbers, you must learn to be responsible and face your challenges head-on rather than succumb to quick-fix solutions, shortcuts, or manipulation. Karmic Debt Number 13/4 brings an opportunity for personal transformation, and when you're honest, patient, and persevere through adversity, you'll overcome this lesson.

Karmic Debt Number 14/5: This number indicates a need to display temperance and moderation in every area of your life and to be mindful of overindulgence. With a 14/5 among your Personality Numbers, you must learn to rise above temptation and earthly desires in favor of responsibility and honoring your commitments. By balancing your desire for freedom and adventure with your responsibilities, you'll overcome this lesson.

Karmic Debt Number 16/7: This number indicates a need to reevaluate your core values and eliminate any superficial foundations that do not align with your higher self. With a 16/7 among your Personality Numbers, you must learn to rise above your ego and pride, treat others with respect, trust and surrender to the unexpected events in your life, and be honest and faithful in love. When you focus on your personal development and rise above your superficial tendencies, you'll overcome this lesson.

Karmic Debt Number 19/1: This number indicates a sense of frustration due to your inability to control everything and everyone in your life. With a 19/1 among your Personality Numbers, you must learn to take others' needs, feelings, and opinions into consideration rather than just your own. By having the courage to accept assistance from others, admitting your mistakes, and seeing others' points of view (regardless of whether they're right or wrong), you'll overcome this lesson.

SUMMARY OF YOUR PERSONALITY NUMBERS

Before we move on to the Personality Number Meanings, let's recap your numbers and what each chart position means:

Life Path Number ______ who you are, your life purpose, the path you will walk in this life.

Destiny Number _______ who you are destined to become as it already resides within you.

Soul Number ______ who your soul desires you to be so it can feel content and complete.

Personality Number ______ how others perceive you.

Maturity Number _______ your future potential, where your life is steering you from 45+.

Birth Day Number ________ additional personality traits, talents and abilities that assist you on your life path.

Current Name Number ________ the vibration you project to the world when you use this name.

Karmic Lesson Numbers _____________ your inherent weaknesses and lessons that must be learned.

Karmic Debt Numbers _________ additional life lessons for numbers 13/4, 14/5, 16/7, 19/1.

Part II

THE PERSONALITY NUMBER MEANINGS

In this section you'll discover the traits, strengths, and challenges of each of the seven Personality Numbers.

Introduction

Before we get to the Personality Number Meanings, here are a couple of points to take into consideration when evaluating your chart and the numerology charts of others:

- The key to an accurate reading lies in blending all of the seven Personality Numbers together.
- Personality Numbers in a chart may contradict each other, so use your common sense. For example: If you have a self-conscious and subservient 2 with a confident and strong-minded 8, you won't be as self-conscious and subservient as a typical 2 would be without the 8.
- Take the person's astrology sign into consideration, as this will influence their personality and the way they express themselves through their numbers. For example: A self-conscious and subservient 2 who has a Leo star sign (a strong and confident leader) won't be as self-conscious and subservient as a typical 2 would be without the Leo influence.
- Take the upbringing and environment into consideration, as this will influence the personality. For example: A confident and strong-minded 8 raised in an abusive

household may not be as confident and strong-minded as a typical 8 would be had they not been exposed to this environment.

- A number has the same meaning wherever it appears, for example: A 7 Life Path Number has the same meaning as a 7 Destiny Number – the only thing that is different is the 'chart position' which has a different meaning.
- There's no such thing as a good or bad number. Each number has positives and negatives, lessons and challenges – and no number is better than another.

Interesting fact

If you lack a positive personality trait that is in any of your numbers, you need to adopt that trait at some stage throughout the course of your life. For example: If you have a 1 or an 8 that is a natural leader, yet you lack this quality, you must adopt leadership abilities at some stage in your life, to fulfill the potential of that number.

Now, let's check out the Personality Number meanings.

Number 1:
The Independent Individual

Number 1's are individual and unique, and often stand out from the crowd. Because they tend to walk a path less traveled, they have their own way of doing things that may not conform to the norm. Their "individuality" and "uniqueness" are their greatest sources of empowerment. They are also the key to their success. When 1's have the courage to be different or to express a different viewpoint without requiring the approval of others, they are well on their way to standing in their full power and improving their quality of life.

Number 1's are self-motivated and self-reliant. They are natural leaders who don't like taking orders and prefer to be in charge. If they can't make their own decisions they may strive toward a position of authority or simply work alone. Many 1's have executive and administration abilities and prefer to be in management or to be self-employed. They are often drawn to innovative and creative fields of employment in which they can initiate projects or assume a leadership role. Life is a journey of self-discovery for all of us, but for 1s, it's their life purpose. Self-awareness, along with an understanding of how they relate to others, is their main area in need of focus in this life.

Interesting fact

When living in the positive, 1's are gifted and innovative thinkers with extremely creative fertile minds. By using creative visualization to direct their powerful thoughts toward the accomplishment of their goals, they can manifest their dreams with greater ease.

Top 5 strengths

- Pioneering
- Courageous
- Innovative
- Self-motivated
- Determined

Top 5 challenges

- Impatient
- Intolerant
- Controlling
- Competitive
- Aggressive

Number 1's make fantastic:

Business owners, managers, supervisors, executives, and team leaders; designers, inventors, creators, and ideas people; life coaches; property and real-estate professionals. 1's are happiest when they're self-employed, work in a position of authority, or work autonomously.

1 Life Path Number

If you have a 1 Life Path Number **you already are** an "Independent Individual" and you will walk that path in this life for it is your life purpose.

1 Destiny Number

If you have a 1 Destiny Number, **you are destined to become** an "Independent Individual" in this life, as it already resides within you.

1 Soul Number

If you have a 1 Soul Number, **your soul longs for you to be** an "Independent Individual" in this life, so it can feel complete.

1 Personality Number

If you have a 1 Personality Number, **you are perceived by others to be** an "Independent Individual."

1 Maturity Number

If you have a 1 Maturity Number, **you are on course to become** an "Independent Individual" from the age of 45+ (or may already be well on your way, if you have reached beyond this age).

1 Current Name Number

If you have a 1 Current Name Number, **you're projecting out the vibration of** an "Independent Individual" every time you use this name.

1 Birth Day Number

If you have a 1 Birth Day Number, **you have personality traits of** Number 1 that can assist you on your life path and help you to fulfill your pre-chosen destiny.

Born on the 1st of the month

If you were born on the 1st, you're a strong individual with leadership abilities. You have a creative and inventive mind that must be utilized. You prefer to be in charge or self-employed. Your independent streak encourages you to march to the beat of your own drum.

Born on the 10th of the month

If you were born on the 10th, you're a natural manager and leader. Highly independent and unique, it's important that you embrace your individuality and originality, because this is the key to your success. You can be competitive and insecure, and like to be number one.

Born on the 19th of the month

If you were born on the 19th, you have executive abilities and are driven to achieve your goals. When you admit your mistakes and accept advice from others, you increase your potential for success. A talented leader, you are often respected by others.

Born on the 28th of the month

If you were born on the 28th, you're a go-getter who doesn't take "no" for an answer. When you have your mind set on something, you'll do everything in your power to get it. You're competitive and like to stand out in a crowd. You combine strength with intuition and compassion.

Number 1 case study

Ever since she was a little girl, Sarah felt like an outsider. She was unusually tall for a girl (and for her age) and the other children would constantly make fun of her, calling her "Beanstalk" or "Giant." This lowered her self-esteem and caused Sarah to spend most of her childhood hiding in the background so she wouldn't stand out in a crowd.

When she was 13, the local championship basketball team came to her school to do a demonstration and to teach the kids how to play. As far as the children were concerned, these players were the heroes of the community and everybody idolized them. It was a pretty big deal that they had chosen to come to their school.

Due to her height, Sarah was chosen out of everybody in the school to learn some of the moves in the demonstration. The team captain chose her personally and praised her for being so tall. He explained her height was an automatic advantage in the world of basketball, providing she had some of the other necessary skills required to succeed. Sarah knew this was a touch-and-go situation where the outcome could go either way.

It took every ounce of courage Sarah had to stand up that day and give playing basketball a go. And it took an extreme amount of willpower to "do her best" while risking even further ridicule. But she did it. And not only did she do it, she nailed it! She blew everyone away with her natural talent and ability for a game she'd never played before. Not only did Sarah discover she was a talented basketball player, she discovered how to use her difference to her advantage. That day, Sarah realized the individuality and uniqueness of being a Number 1 was one of her greatest gifts.

Number 1 meditation

Whether you have a 1 in your numerology chart or not, meditate upon the positive qualities of number 1 that resonate most with you. Imagine yourself adopting those particular traits and visualize them benefiting you in your life. Perhaps you need to be a little more ambitious, proactive, and outgoing? Maybe you need to be more independent so you can stand on your own two feet? Perhaps it will help you further along your path if you can embrace your individuality and uniqueness so you can be your true, authentic self? Maybe you have leadership abilities waiting to be utilized in this life?

Number 2:
The Cooperative Peacemaker

Number 2's are cooperative peacemakers, who have a natural ability to comfort and heal people, animals, and the environment around them. Even though they may be a little insecure and shy until they feel comfortable in their surroundings, they are likeable and genuine, and very easy to get along with. They are natural counselors, who are understanding of people and their problems. This is why they often play a counseling role in their personal lives and/or career.

2's are peaceful and agreeable by nature and will avoid an argument at any costs, often sacrificing their own needs in the process. Therefore, learning to value themselves by putting themselves first is one of their greatest life lessons. Because this doesn't come easily to them, they usually give more than they receive. They may get taken advantage of or end up with the short end of the stick. Once they have the courage to assert themselves and say "no," they are well on their way to standing in their full power and improving their quality of life.

Interesting fact

Number 2's prefer being part of a twosome rather than being on their own, and they thrive when in a mutually loving relationship. They are emotionally sensitive as well as sensitive to negative energy, so they require a healthy and harmonious environment at all times.

Top 5 strengths

- Harmonious
- Intuitive
- Loving
- Supportive
- Understanding

Top 5 challenges

- Moody
- Hypersensitive
- Insecure
- Jealous
- Indecisive

2's make fantastic:

Counselors, mediators, negotiators, and therapists; healers, energy workers, massage therapists, and health professionals; administrators, secretaries, and assistants; teachers, analysts, auditors, and accountants.

2 Life Path Number

If you have a 2 Life Path Number **you already are** a "Co-operative Peacemaker" and you will walk that path in this life, for it is your life purpose.

2 Destiny Number

If you have a 2 Destiny Number, **you are destined to become** a "Cooperative Peacemaker" in this life, as it already resides within you.

2 Soul Number

If you have a 2 Soul Number, **your soul longs for you to be** a "Cooperative Peacemaker" in this life, so it can feel complete.

2 Personality Number

If you have a 2 Personality Number, **you are perceived by others to be** a "Cooperative Peacemaker."

2 Maturity Number

If you have a 2 Maturity Number, **you are on course to become** a "Cooperative Peacemaker" from the age of 45+ (or may already be well on your way, if you have reached beyond this age).

2 Current Name Number

If you have a 2 Current Name Number, **you're projecting out the vibration of** a "Cooperative Peacemaker" every time you use this name.

2 Birth Day Number

If you have a 2 Birth Day Number, **you have personality traits of** Number 2 that can assist you on your life path and help you to fulfill your pre-chosen destiny.

Born on the 2nd of the month

If you were born on the 2nd, you seek balance and harmony in your life. You're cooperative, empathetic, and understanding of others' problems. You work well with others but need to build your self-confidence. Love and partnership are very important to you.

Born on the 20th of the month

If you were born on the 20th, you're a peaceful person who dislikes arguing and confrontation. You're empathetic toward others and are a natural counselor and healer. You can be indecisive and insecure; however, self-confidence is your key to success.

Born on the 11th of the month

(*See Master Number 11/2, page 91*)

Born on the 29th of the month

(*See Master Number 11/2, page 91*)

Number 2 case study

Margaret is a registered nurse, a mother of two, and a Reiki practitioner in her spare time. Always willing to offer a helping hand or a shoulder to cry on, she's the one everybody turns to when they need any type of assistance in their life. Due to her inability to say "no" to a request for help, she would constantly find herself giving healing sessions on her days off, babysitting the neighbor's kids, or preparing the accounts for her brother's business. This left her feeling tired, taken advantage of, and out of balance.

It didn't take long for this rigorous schedule of "giving" to take its toll on her health and Margaret to become bedridden with an illness. Not only did this make her take a step back, but it also forced her to evaluate her health and wellbeing, her behavior, and her life. After several weeks in bed, Margaret recognized where her life was out of balance. She realized that if she wanted to spend her remaining years "happy and healthy" she would need to honor her personal needs and monitor her self-care.

Margaret began by creating a weekly timetable in which she scheduled her essential commitments, such as family obligations and work. Then she added a lot of "free space" for herself. This free space was non-negotiable and had to be used for her happiness and wellbeing, and nothing else. She also cut back on her Reiki healings, told the neighbor she couldn't babysit her kids, and had her brother hire somebody else to prepare his accounts. Not only did this create more balance and personal space and improve her health, it gave her a sense of empowerment that she had never experienced before.

Admittedly, several years later Margaret is still learning to say "no." It doesn't come easy for her and it still takes a lot of courage. However, she has realized her health and happiness are far more important than upsetting others by not doing what they *want her to do. She has finally started to understand that if somebody has a problem with her saying "no," it's their problem, not hers. This has been one of her greatest lessons as a 2.*

Number 2 meditation

Whether you have a 2 in your numerology chart or not, meditate upon the positive qualities of number 2 that resonate most with you. Imagine yourself adopting those particular traits and visualize them benefiting you in your life. Perhaps you need to be a little more balanced, patient, or understanding? Maybe you need to be more caring and nurturing towards others and yourself? Perhaps it will help you further along your path if you could enhance your intuition to receive clear and accurate guidance? Maybe there are times when you could give a little more than you receive?

Number 3: The Self-Expressive Creative

Number 3's are natural entertainers who love to express their many talents and abilities. They have a good sense of humor and enjoy being around people. They're happiest when they're being creative, uplifting, or entertaining an audience - or simply making others laugh. Some 3's are artistically gifted where others are gifted with words (written and/or spoken). However, learning to use their words in a "positive" way to empower and inspire, as opposed to criticize, gossip, or complain, is one of their greatest lessons.

Self-expression - whether it's artistic, kinesthetic, verbal or conceptual - is their key to happiness. When they express themselves using their hands, bodies, words, visions, and ideas, they improve their overall wellbeing and quality of life. Due to the scattered energy of number 3, many 3's can lack discipline and be disorganized, inconsistent, and changeable. Therefore extra effort is required to achieve mental, emotional, physical, and financial stability and order.

Top 5 strengths

- Humorous
- Imaginative
- Creative
- Friendly
- Charismatic

Top 5 challenges

- Scattered
- Critical
- Melodramatic
- Attention-seeking
- Gossipy

Interesting fact

When a 3-person has a number 4 and/or a number 8 among their seven Personality Numbers, they may not be as artistic as a typical 3 would be without a 4 or an 8. It isn't uncommon for the left-brain nature of the 4 and the 8 to diminish the artistic aspect of the 3.

3's make fantastic:

Artists, actors, and entertainers; writers, speakers, and teachers; salespeople, flight attendants, and shop assistants; interior designers, therapists, and chefs; hair, make-up and clothing stylists.

3 Life Path Number

If you have a 3 Life Path Number **you already are** a "Self-expressive Creative" and you will walk that path in this life for it is your life purpose.

3 Destiny Number

If you have a 3 Destiny Number, **you are destined to become** a "Self-expressive Creative" in this life, as it already resides within you.

3 Soul Number

If you have a 3 Soul Number, **your soul longs for you to be** a "Self-expressive Creative" in this life, so it can feel complete.

3 Personality Number

If you have a 3 Personality Number, **you are perceived by others to be** a "Self-expressive Creative."

3 Maturity Number

If you have a 3 Maturity Number, **you are on course to become** a "Self-expressive Creative" from the age of 45+ (or may already be well on your way, if you have reached beyond this age).

3 Current Name Number

If you have a 3 Current Name Number, **you're projecting out the vibration of** a "Self-expressive Creative" every time you use this name.

3 Birth Day Number

If you have a 3 Birth Day Number, **you have personality traits of** Number 3 that can assist you on your life path and help you to fulfill your pre-chosen destiny.

Born on the 3rd of the month

If you were born on the 3rd, you have a good sense of humor and enjoy communicating with others. You may also have artistic or creative abilities. People are attracted to your charismatic personality and you have that "certain something" that cannot be described.

Born on the 12th of the month

If you were born on the 12th, you're sociable and friendly and enjoy being around people. You're a natural entertainer with the ability to cheer people up when they're down. You possess the independence and determination of the 1, with the kindness and compassion of the 2.

Born on the 21st of the month

If you were born on the 21st, you were born with the gift of communication. You're a talented speaker and can talk to anyone about anything; however, you must be mindful not to use your words to gossip or complain. You're multi-talented with varied interests.

Born on the 30th of the month

If you were born on the 30th, you're a born entertainer who likes to be the center of attention. You may be artistically or creatively gifted, or clever with your hands. You're a talented speaker who has a way with words. But you must use your words to uplift, rather than to criticize or put down.

Number 3 case study

As a 3 Life Path child, Soreya was a bubbly little girl who loved to sing, dance, and perform for her family and friends. This was how she expressed herself as a 3 before her life took a turn for the worse. When she was 5, Soreya's light was dimmed when she became the victim of sexual abuse and therein began the conditioning that would play out in her future.

Over the years that followed, Soreya started to express herself in negative ways. She became an attention seeker, acted promiscuously, lived life in the fast lane, and became addicted to alcohol and drugs. By the time she entered her late 20's she had hit rock bottom and had no choice but to face her past and deal with the pain she had tried so desperately to avoid. It was only after enduring a near-death experience and a sexual assault that she finally "woke up."

This turning point propelled Soreya into an intense period of personal development involving various programs, practitioners, conventional and spiritual practices, and transformational modalities. As she started to understand, love, and accept herself, she began to express herself in positive ways. She learned to identify, communicate, and express her feelings through poetry, singing, journaling, writing, and dancing.

As she began to transform herself and her life, she

used her natural talent for communication and self-expression to bring joy, peace, and healing to others through public speaking, teaching, writing, and counseling. Over the years Soreya has used her gifts to heal herself and others. Today she is a popular transformational life coach and workshop facilitator assisting others on their journey toward forgiveness, self-acceptance, and self-love. She runs a successful business, has plenty of time for adventure and fun, and travels the world doing what she loves. Life continues to throw her curve balls, but like a typical number 3, she never stays down for long and nothing will ever dim her light again.

Number 3 meditation

Whether you have a 3 in your numerology chart or not, meditate upon the positive qualities of number 3 that resonate most with you. Imagine yourself adopting those particular traits and visualize them benefiting you in your life. Perhaps you have a project you'd like to pursue and require some additional creative flair? Maybe you need to communicate more effectively with others and learn to speak your truth? Perhaps it would help you further along your path if you could lighten up and have a little more fun? Maybe you have an artistic or creative talent you'd like to enhance?

Number 4: The Dedicated Worker

Number 4's are hard workers who commit themselves to their goals and like to present a high quality of workmanship. They are the cornerstones of any enterprise and their accuracy and attention to detail make them talented auditors, book-keepers, and builders. Even though 4's are extremely logical, practical, and reliable (which are very valuable qualities to have), they could benefit from being a little less serious and thinking outside the box.

As 4's are here to learn how to "overcome and persevere," they often feel held back or restricted in life. However, if any number has the ability to persist through adversity or to overcome a challenge, it's a 4. Number 4's aren't overly emotional and they prefer to keep their thoughts and feelings to themselves. In order to thrive in their personal lives and career, they require emotional, financial, and physical stability. 4's are here to learn to use a step-by-step process to build a solid foundation for their future.

Interesting fact

When a 4 person has a 3 and/or a 5 among their seven Personality Numbers, they are more social, outgoing, and less serious than a typical 4 would be without a 3 or a 5. The scattered and flexible nature of 3 and 5 helps 4 to be less rigid and more adaptable.

Top 5 strengths

- Hardworking
- Organized
- Grounded
- Responsible
- Focused

Top 5 challenges

- Inflexible
- Intolerant
- Stubborn
- Narrow-minded
- Pessimistic

4's make fantastic:

CEO's and managers; accountants, auditors, editors, surveyors and analysts; banking and finance professionals; builders, engineers, architects, and planners; law-enforcement, property, and real-estate professionals.

4 Life Path Number

If you have a 4 Life Path Number **you already are** a "Dedicated Worker" and you will walk that path in this life, for it is your life purpose.

4 Destiny Number

If you have a 4 Destiny Number, **you are destined to become** a "Dedicated Worker" in this life, as it already resides within you.

4 Soul Number

If you have a 4 Soul Number, **your soul longs for you to be** a "Dedicated Worker" in this life, so it can feel complete.

4 Personality Number

If you have a 4 Personality Number, **you are perceived by others to be** a "Dedicated Worker."

4 Maturity Number

If you have a 4 Maturity Number, **you are on course to become** a "Dedicated Worker" from the age of 45+ (or may already be well on your way, if you have reached beyond this age).

4 Current Name Number

If you have a 4 Current Name Number, **you're projecting out the vibration of** a "Dedicated Worker" every time you use this name.

4 Birth Day Number

If you have a 4 Birth Day Number, **you have personality traits of** Number 4 that can assist you on your life path and help you to fulfill your pre-chosen destiny.

Born on the 4th of the month

If you were born on the 4th, you're strong-minded and determined. You set high standards for yourself and others, and honesty is very important to you. You're hard-working and conscientious about the quality of work you present. Others trust and rely on you.

Born on the 13th of the month

If you were born on the 13th, you've had to learn the value of hard work. No stranger to the importance of perseverance and discipline, you're a talented problem-solver who gets things done. You combine the strength and determination of the 1 with the creative mind of the 3.

Born on the 31st of the month

If you were born on the 31st, you're practical and grounded, and blessed with creative ideas. You're conscientious and hard-working, and strive to get results. You work well with others but prefer to be in charge. People respect and admire you, and rely on your advice.

Number 4 case study

David had been an accountant for his entire working life. He had worked for the same company for 16 years and had enjoyed the same daily routine throughout that time, too. He thrived on the safety and security of knowing what was around the corner, and what mattered most to him was having control over everything that happened in his life. He was an expert at making sure everything was "in order" so that it flowed "just right" without any major disruptions or changes.

David took great pride in balancing his clients' accounts and was dedicated to his job. He was a self-confessed workaholic with no social life outside the office. That didn't bother him, because he believed in order to get ahead in life it had to be "all work and no play," which suited him just fine. Fun, friendship, travel, and adventure were things that didn't come onto his radar because, despite feeling lonely, he believed they were simply a waste of time and money.

One morning in 2013, David's world came crashing down when he was made redundant. After applying for several jobs online, he entered therapy to overcome his symptoms of minor depression. Funnily enough, part of his therapy involved taking a well-deserved vacation overseas that forced him to loosen up and have some fun – and to trust that his needs would be met when he returned. This was a concept foreign to David, but he decided to trust his therapist anyway and go. He'd saved a fortune over the years, so this experience helped him to learn it was "healthy and safe" to spend some of the money he'd held onto so tightly.

While on vacation David received an email to say his application for a job with a local company he'd dealt with in the past had been accepted. Shortly after he started work there, he met an auditor who would become his wife. Despite his life being turned upside down, David now knows from experience that sometimes our worst nightmare can be a blessing in disguise. One of the most important things he discovered from the experience was how to have fun and trust in the unknown. He learned that it's healthy (and sometimes necessary) to shake things up in order to create balance. He's very grateful to know that we can't control life - and now understands that sometimes that's a good thing!

Number 4 meditation

Whether you have a 4 in your numerology chart or not, meditate upon the positive qualities of number 4 that resonate most with you. Imagine yourself adopting those particular traits and visualize them benefiting you in your life. Perhaps you need to be a little more disciplined and committed to achieving your goals? Maybe you would benefit from being more logical, practical, and grounded, in order to get things done? Perhaps it would help you further along your path if you could persist through adversity to improve the circumstances of your life? Maybe you could do with being a little more organized in your everyday life?

Number 5: The Freedom-Loving Adventurer

Number 5's are movers and shakers who desire freedom from restrictions and thrive on variety and change. There is never a dull moment for 5's, as their lives are action-packed and constantly filled with change. Multi-talented, adaptable, and versatile, 5's tend to be good at many different things. They may even have different types of jobs throughout their career. Whatever it is they choose to do, they're natural salespeople, consultants, and advisors, with a talent for working with people.

As a typical 5 can have an addictive personality in search of the next high, 5 people have a tendency to overindulge in physical things that pleasure the senses, such as food, alcohol, sex, nicotine, overspending, or over-exercising. Due to their fear of restriction, boredom, or being fenced in, 5's may take a while to commit to a relationship, job, or long-term study program fully. 5's are natural messengers and promoters and they can excel in the area of communication, networking, and PR. Even though they're restless, inconsistent, and easily bored, their charismatic and magnetic personalities make them popular storytellers with the gift of the gab.

Interesting fact

When a 5 person has a number 4 and/or a number 8 among their seven Personality Numbers they are more grounded, responsible, and less addictive than a typical 5 would be without a 4 or 8. The disciplined, focused, and serious nature of 4 and 8 helps to stabilize and anchor the scattered energy of the 5.

Top 5 strengths

- Resourceful
- Multi-talented
- Good communicators
- Adaptable
- Charismatic

Top 5 challenges

- Addictive
- Melodramatic
- Intolerant
- Unfocused
- Changeable

5's make fantastic:

Salespeople, advisors, and consultants; project managers; event planners, promoters, and publicists; investigators, reporters, journalists, and writers; teachers, travel consultants, and flight attendants; hairstylists and public speakers.

5 Life Path Number

If you have a 5 Life Path Number **you already are** a "Freedom-loving Adventurer" and you will walk that path in this life, for it is your life purpose.

5 Destiny Number

If you have a 5 Destiny Number, **you are destined to become** a "Freedom-loving Adventurer" in this life, as it already resides within you.

5 Soul Number

If you have a 5 Soul Number, **your soul longs for you to be** a "Freedom-loving Adventurer" in this life, so it can feel complete.

5 Personality Number

If you have a 5 Personality Number, **you are perceived by others to be** a "Freedom-loving Adventurer."

5 Maturity Number

If you have a 5 Maturity Number, **you are on course to become** a "Freedom-loving Adventurer" from the age of 45+ (or may already be well on your way, if you have reached beyond this age).

5 Current Name Number

If you have a 5 Current Name Number, **you're projecting out the vibration of** a "Freedom-loving Adventurer" every time you use this name.

5 Birth Day Number

If you have a 5 Birth Day Number, **you have personality traits of** Number 5 that can assist you on your life path and help you to fulfill your pre-chosen destiny.

Born on the 5th of the month

If you were born on the 5th, you have the gift of the gab. A born communicator, you can talk to anyone about anything. You're multi-talented and have a variety of interests; however, you're easily bored when something is no longer a challenge. You find it easier to commit to things that mentally stimulate you.

Born on the 14th of the month

If you were born on the 14th, you're a natural communicator and salesperson. You have the gift of the gab and people are attracted to your charismatic personality. Your challenge is to make a commitment and stick with it. Be mindful of addiction and overindulgence.

Born on the 23rd of the month

If you were born on the 23rd, you're a mover and a shaker with a magnetic personality. You like excitement and adventure and need your freedom to do your own thing.

You enjoy networking with others and offering advice. You're a natural salesperson and promoter.

Number 5 case study

Born into a family of accountants, Rachel was expected to follow in her parents' footsteps – and for several years she did. As a 5 Life Path with a 4 Birth Day, she had a razor-sharp mind and a gift for numbers. She made an excellent accountant and her clients loved her to bits, but even though she enjoyed working for the family business, her heart wasn't in it because her real passion lay elsewhere.

Rachel had a passion for cruising the world and she loved to share her experiences with clients, family, and friends. Her natural ability to inspire others to want to do the same was uncanny. In fact, many of the people she knew had booked cruises (and thoroughly enjoyed them) based on her recommendations. What Rachel enjoyed the most about cruising were the shore excursions. To satisfy her adventurous spirit and to get the most out of every location, she would experience as many as possible, and she had a fabulous time doing so. In her little corner of the world, Rachel was the "go to" person for anybody who needed advice on cruising and excursions.

In 2008, the premature death of a friend prompted her to re-evaluate her life and career. She realized life was too short to stay in a job she didn't like simply to keep her parents happy. She knew she had to be true to herself by at least "trying" to fulfill her dream of working on a cruise ship and seeing the world. For several years she studied to obtain the necessary qualifications to apply for her ideal job. For another 18 months after that she constantly networked and promoted herself until she finally got her big break. Today she is the Shore Excursions Director for a major international cruise line, traveling the world and living her dream.

Over the years Rachel has learned to follow the natural energy of her number 5. As a gifted communicator and natural salesperson she has the ability to inspire others through her passion for what she loves. She's the first to admit she has to monitor constantly her 5's desire to overindulge and overspend; however, the self-discipline of her 4 Birth Day Number manages to keep her in line.

Number 5 meditation

Whether you have a 5 in your numerology chart or not, meditate upon the positive qualities of number 5 that resonate most with you. Imagine yourself adopting those particular traits and visualize them benefiting you in your life. Perhaps you need to be a little more outgoing and adventurous so you can experience more of life? Maybe you need a shake-up and to try new things to revitalize your spirit and re-spark a zest for life? Perhaps it would help you further along your path if you could fully embrace your freedom so you can be your true authentic self?

Number 6:
The Responsible Caregiver

Number 6's are natural counselors and advisors, who enjoy being of assistance to others. Whether it's helping a friend to heal a broken heart, nursing a family member back to good health, or helping a neighbor to move house, they love to be of service and thrive when they are needed. If you're ever in need of a helping hand, a shoulder to cry on, or a loyal friend, look no further than a 6. Love relationships, friendships, and family are what matters most to them.

However, 6's can be overachievers and perfectionists who feel as if they're not giving, being, doing, or achieving "enough." Because they give more than they receive, they can be taken for granted or taken advantage of by others. As well as learning to find a healthy balance between giving and receiving, they must also learn the difference between helping and interfering or assisting and enabling those in need. When a 6 balances their own self-care with being of service to others, they live happy, meaningful, and emotionally fulfilled lives.

Interesting fact

Number 6 governs love, friendship, parenting, marriage, and divorce, and 6 people are here to learn lessons in these areas. However, that doesn't mean every 6 is going to marry and divorce, or conceive children. 6 people strive to be their best and want others to do the same, but they must learn that perfect people, relationships, and experiences simply don't exist.

Top 5 strengths

- Nurturing
- Supportive
- Sympathetic
- Loving
- Reliable

Top 5 challenges

- Bossy
- Critical
- Interfering
- Self-righteous
- Perfectionist

6's make fantastic:

Teachers, counselors, and therapists; healers and health practitioners; interior designers and chefs; hair, make-up or clothing stylists; flight attendants and customer service officers; nutritionists, life coaches, and fitness or personal trainers.

6 Life Path Number

If you have a 6 Life Path Number **you already are** a "Responsible Caregiver" and you will walk that path in this life, for it is your life purpose.

6 Destiny Number

If you have a 6 Destiny Number, **you are destined to become** a "Responsible Caregiver" in this life, as it already resides within you.

6 Soul Number

If you have a 6 Soul Number, **your soul longs for you to be** a "Responsible Caregiver" in this life, so it can feel complete.

6 Personality Number

If you have a 6 Personality Number, **you are perceived by others to be** a "Responsible Caregiver."

6 Maturity Number

If you have a 6 Maturity Number, **you are on course to become** a "Responsible Caregiver" from the age of 45+ (or may already be well on your way, if you have reached beyond this age).

6 Current Name Number

If you have a 6 Current Name Number, **you're projecting out the vibration of** a "Responsible Caregiver" every time you use this name.

6 Birth Day Number

If you have a 6 Birth Day Number, **you have personality traits of** Number 6 that can assist you on your life path and help you to fulfill your pre-chosen destiny.

Born on the 6th of the month

If you were born on the 6th, you're reliable and responsible and enjoy taking care of others. People often turn to you for assistance and advice. You're family-orientated and would rather be in a relationship than on your own. Love is very important to you.

Born on the 15th of the month

If you were born on the 15th, you have a magnetic personality and enjoy helping others. Due to the independence of your 1 and your 5's need for freedom, you need the space to be yourself in relationships. Love and family are very important to you.

Born on the 24th of the month

If you were born on the 24th, you are family-orientated and like to be needed. You're a natural parent and caregiver and are happiest when you're helping someone out. You may work in a service-based career but you need to be mindful not to "over help" or interfere in others' lives.

Number 6 case study

Annie is a typical 6 Life Path. She's a dedicated mother of two who loves taking care of her family and she's a substitute teacher at the local elementary school.

She used to teach full-time before she had children of her own, but she retired after the birth of her first child to be a stay-at-home mom. When her youngest started middle school she began teaching part-time so she could still fulfill her obligations as a mother, homemaker, and wife while bringing in some extra cash. Annie's number one priority is to be there for her family, catering to their every need.

As a typical 6, Annie would always put her family's needs above her own to the point of neglecting her own happiness and wellbeing in the process. Even though she was an extremely talented cook with a gift for creating unique and delicious recipes, she believed she couldn't possibly fulfill her dream of having her own catering business before her children left home, because it would mean she was being a selfish and neglectful mom. She felt it wouldn't be fair on her family if she put her own needs first.

When her children were in high school Annie found herself at a crossroads, as she was given a wonderful opportunity to cater for a local café three lunchtimes a week. Even though this was a dream come true and could be accomplished without too much disruption to her duties as a mom, she felt a tremendous amount of guilt about accepting the job. As a 6, one of her life lessons is to learn to balance her home life with her career, and this was a perfect opportunity to do so. After several sleepless nights and heartfelt conversations with her husband, Annie found the courage to give it a go.

Now four years later, Annie believes it was one of the best decisions she's ever made. She feels she's a much better mother and wife because she is happier, as a result of living a more balanced life. She has found a happy medium between catering to her family's needs and fulfilling her own dream at the same time. By working during school hours she can balance motherhood with her career and her family's needs with her own. Now she realizes that it's okay to do something for herself and that just because she has a career it doesn't make her a "terrible mom."

Number 6 meditation

Whether you have a 6 in your numerology chart or not, meditate upon the positive qualities of number 6 that resonate most with you. Imagine yourself adopting those particular traits and visualize them benefiting you in your life. Perhaps you need to take more responsibility for your thoughts and actions so you can achieve your goals with greater ease? Maybe you could be more caring and supportive of the people around you – especially those outside your family and circle of friends? Perhaps it would help you further along your path if you were to offer your services, attention, or time to those in need of a helping hand?

Number 7:
The Contemplative Truth-Seeker

Number 7's are talented problem-solvers and strategists who can excel in psychology, metaphysics, science, engineering, analytics, research, accounting, health, education, philosophy, or technology (especially computers and IT). It will depend on the other 6 Personality Numbers in their numerology chart as to where their natural talents lie. However, one thing all 7's have in common is their desire for knowledge, wisdom, and understanding. Whether it's a desire to understand human behavior, the mechanics of a piece of machinery, or the nature of the universe itself, 7's are always searching for answers and meaning on their quest to seek the truth.

7's need their privacy and "alone time" for introspective thinking and contemplation. Quiet time away from others and the hustle and bustle of life is vital to their wellbeing as it helps to center and ground them. Highly intuitive and perceptive, 7's have an affinity with nature, the ocean, and mother Earth. Mindful practices, such as meditation, yoga, and qi gong, are beneficial for everybody but especially for 7's. The life purpose of number 7 is to discover their spiritual truth from within and to look "beyond the surface" to uncover the secrets and mysteries of the Universe.

Interesting fact

When a 7 person also has a number 3 and/or a 5 among their seven Personality Numbers, is a 34/7 (using the adding-across method, *see page* 6), or has an outgoing astrology sign such as Gemini, Aries, or Leo, they are more social and less withdrawn than a typical 7 would be without those influences. These 7 people integrate more easily with others and require less time alone.

Top 5 strengths

- Intellectual
- Technically orientated
- Investigative
- Intuitive
- Analytical

Top 5 challenges

- Intolerant
- Secretive
- Pessimistic
- Cynical
- Suspicious

7's make fantastic:

Psychiatrists, psychologists, counselors, and therapists; teachers, scientists, and philosophers; investigators, reporters, and journalists; technicians, engineers, accountants, analysts, and strategists; IT consultants and computer programmers; fitness instructors, health and wellbeing practitioners, alternative therapists, and spiritual teachers.

7 Life Path Number

If you have a 7 Life Path Number **you already are** a "Contemplative Truth-seeker" and you will walk that path in this life, for it is your life purpose.

7 Destiny Number

If you have a 7 Destiny Number, **you are destined to become** a "Contemplative Truth-seeker" in this life, as it already resides within you.

7 Soul Number

If you have a 7 Soul Number, **your soul longs for you to be** a "Contemplative Truth-seeker" in this life, so it can feel complete.

7 Personality Number

If you have a 7 Personality Number, **you are perceived by others to be** a "Contemplative Truth-seeker".

7 Maturity Number

If you have a 7 Maturity Number, **you are on course to become** a "Contemplative Truth-seeker" from the age of 45+ (or may already be well on your way, if you have reached beyond this age).

7 Current Name Number

If you have a 7 Current Name Number, **you're projecting out the vibration of** a "Contemplative Truth-seeker" every time you use this name.

7 Birth Day Number

If you have a 7 Birth Day Number, **you have personality traits of** Number 7 that can assist you on your life path and help you to fulfill your pre-chosen destiny.

Born on the 7th of the month

If you were born on the 7th, you have a deep and analytical mind. You dislike superficiality and like to look beyond the surface of things. Quiet time alone away from the hustle and bustle of life is vital to your wellbeing. You're extremely intuitive. Be sure to follow your instincts.

Born on the 16th of the month

If you were born on the 16th, you can see through phony people and situations. You don't trust easily. Deep, contemplative, and intuitive - you look beyond the surface of things. Personal development and a complete overcoming of the ego is the key to your success.

Born on the 25th of the month

If you were born on the 25th, you may be interested in psychology, metaphysics, or philosophy. You need quiet time alone to process your thoughts and contemplate life. You're a natural student and teacher, but you may appear distant or guarded at times.

Number 7 case study

As a 7 Life Path, Nicky was introduced to the secrets and mysteries of the Universe at a very early age. His mother was a theosophist, with a big library of rare books written by ancient philosophers and metaphysics writers who embraced both Eastern and Western teachings. Nicky received an early education in science, philosophy, and religion from the long discussions he would have every Sunday with his mom, so it was only natural that his passion for spirituality and self-awareness blossomed by the time he reached his teens.

Both of Nicky's parents were alternative and open-minded thinkers who encouraged him not to take the words of authority, educators, doctors, and teachers as gospel. They encouraged him to dig beneath the surface of conventional wisdom, to step outside the box and look deeper at his own personal truth as well. This enabled Nicky successfully to balance intuition with the conventional and spiritual worlds. Even though his different way of thinking caused him to feel alienated in the outer world, he felt completely at peace, safe, and loved in his inner world and at home.

At school, Nicky excelled in science and mathematics, and loved helping people. He later trained to be a primary-school teacher but found it boring, so he studied psychology at university on the side. It didn't take long for psychology to become his passion and, despite being dyslexic, he excelled in his studies. Over the following years he graduated with an M.A. and Ph.D. in Psychology, and a Diploma in Teaching. He also became a Professor of Psychology at a major university overseas while maintaining a clinical and counseling practice.

Nicky was successful in his career because he combined conventional psychology teachings with ancient mystical teachings for the purpose of empowering his clients and students. Now in his 70's, Nicky is the author of five books about spirituality and transformation. He's a public speaker, workshop facilitator, and a self-empowerment mentor to people all over the world. As each year passes, his number 7's passion for spirituality has only grown stronger, and the more wisdom he shares, the more wisdom is made available through his works. If you were to ask Nicky what has given him most satisfaction in life, he'd say, "To have empowered others and to have discovered the fathomless peace of being at home with myself."

Number 7 meditation

Whether you have a 7 in your numerology chart or not, meditate upon the positive qualities of number 7 that resonate most with you. Imagine yourself adopting those particular traits and visualize them benefiting you in your life. Perhaps you would benefit from taking up meditation while you work on improving yourself? Maybe you need to spend more quiet time alone in contemplation, away from the hustle and bustle of life? Perhaps it would help you further along your path if you were to uncover the meaning of life and discover your spiritual truth?

Number 8:
The Business-Minded Leader

There are two types of Number 8's – those who are positive about money and are drawn to self-employment, the business world, and money-making ventures ... and those who have self-sabotaging or limiting beliefs regarding money and personal achievement. It all depends on the other 6 Personality Numbers in their numerology chart as to which direction they will take. Every 8 has the ability to attract abundance and success, but it all depends on their attitude.

As 8 is the number of "money and manifestation," 8's must learn to adopt an attitude of abundance in order to attract it into their lives. 8's are strongly governed by the Law of Attraction and the Law of Cause and Effect, which means it is important that they live honestly and have a positive mindset about life, because their very powerful minds will attract whatever they "think" and "believe." This is the case for every human being, but it is doubly so for number 8's.

Interesting fact

All 8's are here to learn about "personal power." Some must learn not to take other people's power away by being overpowering, manipulative, or controlling – and others must learn not to allow themselves to become disempowered by allowing their power to be taken away.

Top 5 strengths

- Organized
- Self-motivated
- Driven
- Strong
- Hardworking

Top 5 challenges

- Domineering
- Poverty-conscious
- Intimidating
- Superficial
- Manipulative

8's make fantastic:

Business owners, CEO's, supervisors, and managers; banking, finance, and legal professionals; property developers and real-estate professionals; project managers and corporate executives. Most 8's prefer to work in positions of authority or to be self-employed.

8 Life Path Number

If you have an 8 Life Path Number **you already are** a "Business-minded Leader" and you will walk that path in this life, for it is your life purpose.

8 Destiny Number

If you have an 8 Destiny Number, **you are destined to become** a "Business-minded Leader" in this life, as it already resides within you.

8 Soul Number

If you have an 8 Soul Number, **your soul longs for you to be** a "Business-minded Leader" in this life, so it can feel complete.

8 Personality Number

If you have an 8 Personality Number, **you are perceived by others to be** a "Business-minded Leader."

8 Maturity Number

If you have an 8 Maturity Number, **you are on course to become** a "Business-minded Leader" from the age of 45+ (or may already be well on your way, if you have reached beyond this age).

8 Current Name Number

If you have an 8 Current Name Number, **you're projecting out the vibration of** a "Business Minded Leader" - every time you use this name.

8 Birth Day Number

If you have an 8 Birth Day Number, **you have personality traits of** Number 8 that can assist you on your life path and help you to fulfill your pre-chosen destiny.

Born on the 8th of the month

If you were born on the 8th, you're a leader rather than a follower. You have a logical, practical mind and a talent for business. You have the ability to be self-employed or a manager, a supervisor, or a team leader. Your appearance and your achievements are important to you.

Born on the 17th of the month

If you were born on the 17th, you prefer to work in a position of authority. You combine the leadership qualities of your number 1 with the logic and intuition of your 7, making you a talented decision-maker to whom others look for guidance.

Born on the 26th of the month

If you were born on the 26th, you make a good leader because you lead alongside others, as opposed to controlling from above. You're determined and strong-minded, and you don't like being told what to do. You have a talent for business and thrive in self-employment.

Number 8 case study

William discovered early on in his career that he was better off working for himself. As a typical 8 Life Path, he enjoyed the freedom of working his own hours and not having to take orders from anyone.

He worked in a variety of sole-trader positions, but it was when he became an independent real-estate agent that the big money started to roll in. A short while later he'd made enough money to buy himself a lovely new house complete with a shiny new car. He was living the life of Riley and was recognized by the community for his achievements.

Before long, William realized he'd become addicted to money and success. He started working only for the "gold and glory" rather than for his love for the job. He found himself trapped in a vicious circle but he didn't know how to get out. Shortly after reaching this conclusion an unforeseen property slump forced him out of business and his empire came crashing down. William lost his home, his shiny new car, and the glory of status and success. Even though his reversal of fortune caused him to hit rock bottom, William genuinely believes it was the best thing that could have happened to him.

In the months following the crash, William began to re-evaluate himself and his life. Although he was distraught, he was still able to recognize that he didn't like the person he'd become. He realized that his love of money, status, and success had brought out the worst in him and he knew it was for his own good that it had been taken away.

Over time, he began to appreciate the opportunity to reinvent himself and start again. Typically hardworking and confident, and a natural self-starter, it didn't take him long to rebuild another real-estate business.

However, this time he only works for the love of the job. His number one priority is to help his clients find a suitable home and he takes great pleasure in fulfilling their needs. He mentors up-and-coming agents every now again and hosts the odd free seminar on how to make money – the right way! He feels he's a much better person than he was before and, funnily enough, he's making more money now, too!

Number 8 meditation

Whether you have an 8 in your numerology chart or not, meditate upon the positive qualities of number 8 that resonate most with you. Imagine yourself adopting those particular traits and visualize them benefiting you in your life. Perhaps you need to be a little more decisive and courageous when making decisions? Maybe you could adopt an attitude of abundance, so you can become financially safe and secure? Perhaps it would further you along your path to reclaim your personal power from the people and limiting beliefs that have caused you to feel disempowered in some way? Maybe you would benefit from being a leader or a self-starter, or from being self-employed?

Number 9: The Compassionate Humanitarian

Number 9's are compassionate, understanding, and kind - and those that aren't are here to learn to be. Empathetic and generous by nature, they are often drawn to helping others or working in a career of service. As one of their life lessons is to develop broad-mindedness, they will encounter a wide variety of experiences and come into contact with a diverse range of people, from all walks of life. These people and experiences will teach them patience, understanding, and tolerance, and how to be less judgmental.

Many 9's (but not all) are creatively gifted. Some are talented painters, writers, designers, actors, or musicians, whereas others simply have an appreciation of the arts. It isn't uncommon for a 9 to excel in the area of health, education, government, politics, or social welfare. A 9's happiness is found in the act of giving and selfless service, although some 9's accomplish this more easily than others. 9 is ruled by the fiery planet Mars, which is why 9's can also be passionate, emotional, and intense - with a fiery temper to match. Generous by nature, they find joy in showering friends and loved ones with gifts.

Interesting fact

You'll often find a 9 fighting for a worthwhile cause, whether it's the environment, animal or human rights, or supporting a national or international campaign. Number 9's like to fight for the underdog and they want to contribute toward making the world a better place. Some 9's are disappointed in human beings but are extremely passionate about helping animals or the environment.

Top 5 strengths

- Compassionate
- Generous
- Passionate
- Broad-minded
- Sympathetic

Top 5 challenges

- Unforgiving
- Revengeful
- Defensive
- Melodramatic
- Aggressive

9's make fantastic:

Teachers, counselors, and therapists; social workers and health professionals; politicians, activists, and environmentalists; government workers and lawyers; artists, writers, actors, musicians, photographers, and designers; HR and recruitment consultants; and personal trainers and fitness instructors.

9 Life Path Number

If you have a 9 Life Path Number **you already are** a "Compassionate Humanitarian" and you will walk that path in this life, for it is your life purpose.

9 Destiny Number

If you have a 9 Destiny Number, **you are destined to become** a "Compassionate Humanitarian" in this life, as it already resides within you.

9 Soul Number

If you have a 9 Soul Number, **your soul longs for you to be** a "Compassionate Humanitarian" in this life, so it can feel complete.

9 Personality Number

If you have a 9 Personality Number, **you are perceived by others to be** a "Compassionate Humanitarian."

9 Maturity Number

If you have a 9 Maturity Number, **you are on course to become** a "Compassionate Humanitarian" from the age of 45+ (or may already be well on your way, if you have reached beyond this age).

9 Current Name Number

If you have a 9 Current Name Number, **you're projecting out the vibration of** a "Compassionate Humanitarian" every time you use this name.

9 Birth Day Number

If you have a 9 Birth Day Number, you have personality traits of Number 9 that can assist you on your life path and help you to fulfill your pre-chosen destiny.

Born on the 9th of the month

If you were born on the 9th, you have a sensitive and generous nature. You're broad-minded and able to see the bigger picture in life. You've been gifted with the ability to understand a diverse range of people and their cultures. You may also be creatively talented in some way.

Born on the 18th of the month

If you were born on the 18th, you may work in a service-based career. You're a strong-minded and independent person who prefers to be in charge; however, you also have a good understanding of people and their needs. Patience and tolerance are the keys to your success.

Born on the 27th of the month

If you were born on the 27th, you may be artistic or creative. You love to fight for the underdog and have a strong sense of justice. You combine the analytical mind of your number 7 with the intuition of your number 2 – giving you a leading edge when dealing with business matters and people.

Number 9 case study

Ever since the age of nine when she saw an advert about domestic violence on TV, Wendy wanted to help battered wives and children. She herself had suffered years of mental abuse from her father and had witnessed her mother being physically abused by him until he eventually ran off with another woman. When she discovered there were organizations in the community that assisted women and children in need, she was inspired to make working for them her career.

That advert sparked a passion that has remained for 32 years and continues to this day. Over those 32 years Wendy has worked as a counselor at a women's refuge center and a social worker within her community. She loves her job and takes great pleasure in assisting people in need. She is very compassionate toward those who are unable to help themselves and believes the reason she's so good at her job is because she's lived through it herself.

Even though she is passionate about her work, it hasn't always been easy. Regardless of how many tragedies she has witnessed, she has never numbed to the pain and she still finds it hard to accept some of the misfortune in the world. Every day she has to make an effort not to let the adversities of life or other people's pain consume her. Training to be a counselor and a social worker had its challenges, too. It forced her to take a look at her own life and address some of the negative beliefs she had relating to men, relationships, and trust.

If you were to ask her what's been the hardest lesson of her life to date, she'd tell you it's "forgiveness." Wendy feels learning to forgive her father was the hardest thing she's ever had to do, yet at the same time it was the most rewarding. She believes this was the only thing that set her free and she shares this wisdom with her clients and patients every day. Spoken like a true 9, Wendy says, "Without a doubt, above all else, acceptance and forgiveness of the past are the keys to creating a better future."

Number 9 meditation

Whether you have a 9 in your numerology chart or not, meditate upon the positive qualities of number 9 that resonate most with you. Imagine yourself adopting those particular traits and visualize them benefiting you in your life. Perhaps you need to be more compassionate and less judgmental toward others? Maybe you need to be a little more accepting and forgiving of the misfortunes in your life? Perhaps it would help you further along your path to be of service to others and/or the community by offering your attention, services, money, or time?

Master Numbers 11/2, 22/4, and 33/6

Master Numbers 11/2, 22/4, and 33/6 are higher-octave vibrations of the lower base numbers 2, 4, and 6, and they indicate great potential to attain self-mastery during the course of this life. Those with a Master Number 11/2, 22/4, or 33/6 Life Path, Destiny, Soul, or Maturity Number are old souls who have accumulated much spiritual wisdom in previous lives.

Those with a Master Number have free will to decide whether they'll utilize this wisdom in their current lives to help others and contribute to raising the collective consciousness of planet Earth or reject the responsibility and simply live as their base number 2, 4, or 6.

Here are some Interesting facts about people with Master Numbers:

- They have potent energies vibrating at higher frequencies.
- They have chosen to come back to make a difference in some way.

- They must overcome the lower tendencies of their base number 2, 4, or 6 before they can utilize their Master Number potential.
- They may not begin to utilize their Master Number potential until the age of 45+.
- Since they have free will they can choose not to utilize their Master Number potential at all.
- They may be intuitive and have psychic gifts.
- They must be confident, balanced, and grounded to reach their full psychic potential.
- They may suffer from anxiety, extreme sensitivity, and/or low self-esteem.
- They are powerful creators who are strongly governed by the universal laws.
- They may experience many tests, trials, and tribulations, and lead complicated lives.
- They must learn to live with honesty and integrity.
- They have the ability to master a skill.
- They are able to inspire others and transform lives.
- They are on a journey of personal transformation and spiritual enlightenment.
- They particularly benefit from regular meditation, exercise, and a healthy diet.

Now let's take a look at each Master Number individually.

Number 11/2: The Inspirational Teacher

Master Number 11/2 is a higher vibration of Number 2, so it incorporates everything that Number 2 represents along with the added extras of the Number 11. One of these is the ability to uplift and inspire others. As 11/2 is also the number of "illumination," 11/2 people are often on a journey of personal development to discover who they are and to find their own truth. Once this has been accomplished, they pass their wisdom on to others to help them become illuminated, too.

11/2's are considered the most intuitive of all the numbers. Charismatic, sensitive, and enthusiastic, 11/2's run on high-voltage nervous energy. Learning to harness, ground, and balance this nervous energy is one of their greatest challenges. When an 11/2 can master their sensitivity, maintain a healthy level of self-esteem, and overcome the major life lessons of Number 2, they begin to step into the full Master Number power of the 11/2.

(*See also Number 2, page 39*)

Interesting fact

Self-understanding is vital to the success of 11/2's, and they must learn to take responsibility for the role they play in the things that happen in their lives. They must be honest with respect to their actions and intentions, and live by their higher ideals rather than manipulate people (or the truth) to get their own way. Through many tests, trials, and tribulations, they learn about life and accept it in a philosophical manner.

Top 5 strengths

- Intuitive
- Broad-minded
- Inspirational
- Uplifting
- Peacemaker

Top 5 challenges

- Insecure
- Dishonest
- Intense
- Delusional
- Hypersensitive

11/2's make fantastic:

Counselors and therapists; public and motivational speakers; actors, artists, entertainers, athletes, and musicians; politicians and public figures; life coaches, clairvoyants, healers, spiritual teachers, and alternative practitioners; business owners, managers, and entrepreneurs; inventors and visionaries; film and TV producers and directors.

11/2 Life Path Number

If you have an 11/2 Life Path Number **you already are** an "Inspirational Teacher" and you will walk that path in this life, for it is your life purpose.

11/2 Destiny Number

If you have an 11/2 Destiny Number, you are destined to become an "Inspirational Teacher" in this life, as it already resides within you.

11/2 Soul Number

If you have an 11/2 Soul Number, **your soul longs for you to be** an "Inspirational Teacher" in this life, so it can feel complete.

11/2 Personality Number

If you have an 11/2 Personality Number, **you are perceived by others to be** an "Inspirational Teacher."

11/2 Maturity Number

If you have an 11/2 Maturity Number, **you are on course to become** an "Inspirational Teacher" from the age of 45+

(or may already be well on your way, if you have reached beyond this age).

11/2 Current Name Number

If you have an 11/2 Current Name Number, **you're projecting out the vibration of** an "Inspirational Teacher" every time you use this name.

11/2 Birth Day Number

If you have an 11/2 Birth Day Number, **you have personality traits of** Number 11/2 that can assist you on your life path and help you to fulfill your pre-chosen destiny.

Born on the 11th of the month

If you were born on the 11th, you're highly sensitive and intuitive. You're a deep and caring person who enjoys uplifting and inspiring others. You can be easily hurt and taken advantage of by others. When you believe in yourself you can achieve big things.

Born on the 29th of the month

If you were born on the 29th, you're deep, intuitive, and spiritual. You may have an interest in metaphysics or anything that falls under the "mind, body, spirit" umbrella. You're a gifted counselor and healer with an open, loving heart; however, you need to learn to love and appreciate yourself.

Number 11/2 case study

Even as a child Blake had the ability to light up a room. As an 11/2 Life Path he had a bubbly and outgoing personality, despite having been raised in a dramatic family environment. By the time he was five and before his father left home and was barely seen again, he'd witnessed drug addiction, crime, infidelity, and the bitter divorce of his parents. It's not surprising then that, by the time he had reached 15, Blake had learned to cover his pain with a combination of alcohol and drugs that would eventually ruin his life.

At the age of 17, Blake had everything going for him. He was the captain of his varsity football team with an offer to play Division 2 university football; a beautiful girlfriend who loved him; status and respect in the community; and a circle of friends who admired him – yet he was addicted to alcohol and drugs and was dealing drugs on the side. One night while high, he passed out in his car at a "stop" sign and was arrested for "driving under the influence". In the blink of an eye he lost everything. He was kicked off the football team, his girlfriend left him, he was shamed in the community, he was a disgrace to his family, and he lost his self-confidence, his life, and his identity as well.

Going from hero to outcast overnight automatically catapulted him onto a long and challenging journey of self-awareness that uncovered a long-standing lack of self-love and self-worth. On his quest to obtain unconditional self-love, clarity of purpose, healing, and peace, Blake studied at five different universities, exploring various forms of alternative medicine, healing, and spiritual discipline over the course of several years. He also studied practices such as meditation, qi gong, tai chi, and yoga with spiritual masters from China,

Korea, and the USA. When he eventually found the answer to healing himself and fulfilling his purpose, he felt it was his responsibility to share with others what he himself had been blessed to learn. Like a true 11/2, Blake then dedicated the rest of his life to uplifting, empowering, illuminating, and inspiring others to do the same.

As a Master Number, Blake hasn't found his journey easy. He's had countless disappointments and has suffered rejection from dozens of publishers and agents – but he has never ever given up. His passion for illuminating and empowering others has enabled him to persevere through adversity and he has thrived as a result. Today, he is the author of a number-one bestselling self-help book on Amazon Kindle in Australia and he's living his dream. Blake strongly believes his life had to play out the way it did because it helped him create a level of self-love, gain confidence, and earn respect for all he's overcome and achieved – things he might never have experienced otherwise. When he teaches his students that our greatest challenges are often our greatest blessings in disguise, he's teaching from personal experience.

Number 11/2 meditation

Whether you have an 11/2 in your numerology chart or not, meditate upon the positive qualities of number 11/2 that resonate most with you. Imagine yourself adopting those particular traits and visualize them benefiting you in your life. Perhaps you would like to uplift and inspire the people around you? Maybe you feel the need to heal others or raise spiritual awareness on planet Earth? Perhaps it would help you further along your path if you were to live with honesty and integrity and take responsibility for your actions? Maybe you could benefit from taking up mindfulness practices?

Number 22/4:
The Master Builder

Master Number 22/4 is a higher vibration of Number 4 so it incorporates everything that Number 4 represents, along with the added extras of the Number 22. One of those added extras is the gift of vision and the ability to turn dreams into reality through practical application. 22/4's can see the bigger picture of what needs to be done to improve the overall functioning of a business, organization, product, service, project, movement, community - or humanity as a whole.

Number 22/4's are driven to build, develop, create, or promote something of benefit to all by bridging the spiritual and material worlds and applying their practicality and logic with their inner knowing and intuition. 22/4's are natural leaders who have the ability to reach great heights within their chosen field, whether it's the corporate, scientific, health, technological, political, creative, humanitarian, or metaphysical arena. When a 22/4 can master their sensitivity and insecurity, override their fear of failure, and overcome the major life lessons of Number 4, they begin to step into the full Master Number power of the 22/4.

(*See also Number 4, page 51*)

Interesting fact

Despite the 22/4's enormous potential for success, their fear of failure may cause them to abort their hopes and dreams. When they overcome their inferiority complex and trust in others enough to allow them to contribute to their goals and dreams, 22/4's have much potential for success.

Top 5 strengths

- Visionary
- Forward-thinking
- Dedicated
- Focused
- Idealistic

Top 5 challenges

- Inflexible
- Workaholic
- Stubborn
- Controlling
- Perfectionist

22/4's make fantastic:

Business owners, CEO's and managers; public speakers, politicians, and spiritual leaders; inventors, designers, scientists, and engineers; doctors and health practitioners; alternative therapists; environmentalists and public figures.

22/4 Life Path Number

If you have a 22/4 Life Path Number **you already are** a "Master Builder" and you will walk that path in this life, for it is your life purpose.

22/4 Destiny Number

If you have a 22/4 Destiny Number, **you are destined to become** a "Master Builder" in this life, as it already resides within you.

22/4 Soul Number

If you have a 22/4 Soul Number, **your soul longs for you to be** a "Master Builder" in this life, so it can feel complete.

22/4 Personality Number

If you have a 22/4 Personality Number, **you are perceived by others to be** a "Master Builder."

22/4 Maturity Number

If you have a 22/4 Maturity Number, **you are on course to become** a "Master Builder" from the age of 45+ (or may already be well on your way, if you have reached beyond this age).

22/4 Current Name Number

If you have a 22/4 Current Name Number, **you're projecting out the vibration of** a "Master Builder" every time you use this name.

22/4 Birth Day Number

If you have a 22/4 Birth Day Number, **you have personality traits of** Number 22/4 that can assist you on your life path and help you to fulfill your pre-chosen destiny.

Born on the 22nd of the month

If you were born on the 22nd, you're highly sensitive and intuitive. You have the gift of added insight when you combine your intuition with your logical mind. You work well with others and have the ability to lead large projects when you focus and apply yourself.

Number 22/4 case study

From an early age, Janice wanted to be a missionary so she could help the underprivileged in developing countries. As a 22/4 Destiny, she was born with a passion for helping others. The rejection of her application by her church led her into child nursing instead, where she was educated in both Maori and European herbal medicine and traditional ways of healing. During her time as a hospital staff nurse she experienced challenges in using traditional treatments and witnessed a major shift in the medical system as it left traditional forms of healing behind in favor of prescription drug treatments during the 1960's and 70's.

Upon witnessing the negative effects of drugs and the manipulative ways of pharmaceutical corporations, and rather than toe the line and succumb to the new medical model, she left to nurse overseas and further her studies in natural forms of healing. She went on to play a major role in her new community through her volunteer work and running various youth groups, while raising a family, and she also continued to help the community back home. Her passion for natural medicine and the environment grew and before long she had established a very successful practice, complete with herbal gardens, a clinic, an education facility and a green pharmacy dispensary, which soon caused conflict with those entrenched in the new medical model.

Over the years Janice launched two successful national health and holistic publications, which grew into international magazines. She has written two books and countless booklets educating people on health, healing, and environmental issues, which led to a Women in Business Award. She has received an international honorary doctorate for her work, reported international research on major drug complaints, worked with the government of New Zealand to ensure that the country remains independent of international regulatory pharmaceutical control, and has prevented the patenting of herbs in the southern hemisphere through her charitable trust.

Like a true Master 22/4 she has dedicated her life to being a whistleblower who rattles cages to help the community and humanity adopt holistic health principles. Even when various health authorities and corporate organizations legally and illegally threatened her, she stood firm and won the overall battle. Every step of the way, she held her vision and took practical steps to manifest it in reality. Janice believes natural medicine and education are the keys to better health and her wish is that people return to pooling their own natural resources, herbal treatments, and healthy food collectively - free from corporate control. And so far she's doing a pretty good job.

Number 22/4 meditation

Whether you have a 22/4 in your numerology chart or not, meditate upon the positive qualities of number 22/4 that resonate most with you. Imagine yourself adopting those particular traits and visualize them benefiting you in your life. Perhaps you'd like to be involved in something that helps the community or aids humanity as a whole? Maybe you'd like to be a practical visionary who sees what needs to be done to make the world a better place - then take steps toward making it happen? Perhaps it would help you further along your path if you could be more disciplined, organized, and focused? Maybe there is a cause, a product, or a service you'd like to support that will assist others in some way?

Number 33/6: The Master Healer

Master Number 33/6 is a higher vibration of Number 6, so people with this number incorporate everything that Number 6 represents along with the added extras of the Number 33. One of those added extras is the ability to heal others either through conventional or alternative means. Some 33/6's heal through a medical- or health-related platform, as a psychiatrist or a doctor would do, whereas others heal through their self-expression or creativity, in the way in which an entertainer, an artist, or a singer would do.

Due to having a double dose of the self-expressive and creative energy of Number 3, many 33/6's possess artistic abilities. Positive forms of self-expression are very important for their overall wellbeing. Because of the presence of number 6, 33/6's are natural teachers, too. Even though at times they can feel burdened by their responsibilities, their life purpose is to evolve through selfless service to others. When a 33/6 can master their perfectionism, find a healthy balance between giving and receiving, and overcome the major life lessons of Number 6, they begin to step into the full Master Number power of the 33/6.

(*See also Number 6, page 63*).

Interesting fact

Master numerologists believe a genuine 33/6 Life Path Number can only be obtained using the 'Reducing-down' calculation method (*see page* 7). When a 33 is calculated using the 'Adding-across' method (*see page* 6), they will reduce it down to a regular 6. There are also numerologists who don't believe the Master Number 33/6 even exists, choosing only to acknowledge 11/2 and 22/4 as Master Numbers.

Top 5 strengths

- Creative
- Healing
- Compassionate
- Loving
- Nurturing

Top 5 challenges

- Perfectionist
- Overachieving
- Critical
- Self-righteous
- Self-critical

33/6's make fantastic:

Counselors, therapists, and health professionals; child-care professionals, teachers, caregivers, and human rights activists; actors, entertainers, artists, writers, and musicians; designers and decorators; healers, intuitive readers, and alternative therapists.

33/6 Life Path Number

If you have a 33/6 Life Path Number **you already are** a "Master Healer" and you will walk that path in this life, for it is your life purpose.

33/6 Destiny Number

If you have a 33/6 Destiny Number, **you are destined to become** a "Master Healer" in this life, as it already resides within you.

33/6 Soul Number

If you have a 33/6 Soul Number, **your soul longs for you to be** a "Master Healer" in this life, so it can feel complete.

33/6 Personality Number

If you have a 33/6 Personality Number, **you are perceived by others to be** a "Master Healer."

33/6 Maturity Number

If you have a 33/6 Maturity Number, **you are on course to become** a "Master Healer" from the age of 45+ (or may already be well on your way, if you have reached beyond this age).

33/6 Current Name Number

If you have a 33/6 Current Name Number, **you're projecting out the vibration of** a "Master Healer" every time you use this name.

33/6 case study

Ever since she was a little girl Maxine had wanted to be a mother and a children's doctor. Married at the age of 21 and a mother at the age of 25, parenting came naturally to her. She was the happiest she'd ever been taking care of her kids. After the birth of her second child she suffered a medical condition that prevented her from having any more children. This was extremely shocking and devastating for Maxine because she'd envisaged having a large family and being a mother of many.

Once she had accepted her fate, she asked herself, "If I can't have any more children of my own, what can I do to serve other children in need?" Not long afterward she began doing respite care for children with medical problems. She also worked as an integration aid in primary schools. Naturally intuitive with a strong spiritual understanding, Maxine discovered while doing this work that there was a gap in the conventional child wellbeing system that catered for all the children's needs, whether energetic, psychological, or medical. That was when she decided to do a degree in psychology and philosophy (which led to a doctorate in philosophy), so she could create a system of her own.

After years of study, Maxine created a new model for children's wellbeing needs for educators, practitioners, parents, and caregivers that is based on the chakra system. This groundbreaking holistic system integrates mind, body, and spirit and is the only system she could find that accounts for the multi-dimensionality or totality of a child's experiences. In 2014, she received a publication deal based on her doctoral research and created the world's first deck of children's wellbeing cards. She also produced a children's wellbeing chart and a related book, and trained her very own international team of practitioners.

The life of a master number isn't easy and Maxine's is no exception. Throughout her entire journey of selflessly serving others, she has struggled with scleroderma, a rare autoimmune disease that effects the collagen throughout the body and hardens the skin (as a form of self-protection from pain), as well as thyroid cancer and Hashimoto's disease. But like the seeker and trooper that she is, Maxine is miraculously healing her body from the inside out as she peels away layers of her personality and her life. She is certainly someone to watch out for, as her work continues to heal, empower, and transform the children of today - our leaders of the future.

Number 33/6 meditation

Whether you have a 33/6 in your numerology chart or not, meditate upon the positive qualities of number 33/6 that resonate most with you. Imagine yourself adopting and integrating specific 33/6 traits that will benefit you in your life.

Perhaps you have a creative gift that can benefit others in some way? Maybe you'd like to be a healer with an ability to ease another's pain? Perhaps it would further your path if you were to teach, heal, or counsel those who require your assistance? Maybe you have a service, product, or idea you'd like to introduce to the world that benefits others in some way?

Part III

THE FORECASTING NUMBERS

In this section you'll discover the short and long term cycles that influence the circumstances of your life.

Introduction

Like the seasons in a year, your life is divided into seasons, too. In fact, your life is an ongoing pattern of cycles designed for your personal growth. In numerology, each cycle has its own unique theme with specific experiences you may encounter within that period of time. As some cycles are more favorable than others for achieving certain goals, it pays to know which cycle you're in so you're fully aware of the opportunities and challenges you may experience during this period of time. In other words, when it comes to forecasting your future, numerology provides the gift of "added insight" so you know what lies ahead and can be better prepared.

When you understand and surrender to the natural rhythm of your cycles, life becomes a heck of a lot easier because *you're in the flow of life*. Now, you may not be able to avoid life's challenges altogether, but when you know that there's trouble ahead, you're better placed to navigate your way around it. Even though numerology isn't so specific that it can predict the actions you will take when faced with certain circumstances, it will provide an accurate indication of what the circumstances themselves may be, so you know what to expect. This is valuable information that keeps you one step ahead of the game.

Interesting fact

A Forecasting Number has the same meaning wherever it appears. For example – A 7 Personal Year Number has the same meaning as a 7 Personal Month, a 7 Pinnacle, or a 7 Major Life Cycle – the only thing that is different is the chart "position", which has a slightly different meaning.

Within the Forecasting Numbers, there are *short-term cycles* that are more obvious in terms of influencing your life directly – and there are *long-term cycles* overriding them. The long-term cycles may not be as obvious because they extend over a longer period of time.

The short- and long-term Forecasting Numbers we'll be discussing in this book are as follows:

- Personal Year Number: Your forecast for the year (short-term)
- Personal Month Number: Your forecast for the month (short-term)
- Personal Day Number: Your forecast for the day (short-term)
- Universal Year Number: The world's forecast for the year (short-term)
- Universal Month Number: The world's forecast for the month (short-term)

- Universal Day Number: The world's forecast for the day (short-term)
- Pinnacles: Your four cycles of potential achievement (long-term)
- Challenges: Your four greatest challenges (long-term)
- Major Life Cycles: Your three major cycles of growth (long-term)

Let's begin with the Personal Year Number, the first short-term cycle in your chart.

Personal Year Numbers and Their Meanings

Every year you have a Personal Year Number between 1 and 9 that indicates the lessons, opportunities, and experiences you'll encounter during the course of the year. This cycle runs from January 1st to December 31st to coincide with the calendar year. However, sometimes the influence of the upcoming Personal Year Number can be felt several months before the official changeover date on January 1st.

Your Personal Year Number cycle commences at birth and progresses through nine-year intervals throughout your life. Each of the nine years has its own unique theme with respect to the types of lessons and experiences you'll encounter for that year. In comparison with your other forecasting numbers (cycles), your Personal Year Number has the most obvious influence over your life for the year.

When you know your Personal Year Number, you can prepare for what's ahead. This number is a great indicator of the ideal time to take certain actions, such as focusing on your career, moving house, traveling or embarking on an adventure, repairing or beginning a relationship, studying, getting married, working on your personal development, or starting a family. When you know the Personal Year Number of those around you, you'll have a better understanding of what's going on in their lives, too, which can only improve your relationships.

Interesting fact

Some numerologists believe the Personal Year Number runs from birthday to birthday each year. However, as the Personal Year Number relates to the influence the calendar year has upon your life – and the calendar year runs from January 1st to December 31st – the *Personal Year* cycle must also run from January 1st to December 31st. That being said, the influence of your Personal Year tends to be stronger from your birthday onward.

How to calculate the Personal Year Number

Step 1: Add the *month* and *day* of your birth date to the current calendar year.

Step 2: Add any double-digit numbers together to get a single-digit Personal Year Number between 1 and 9. For example, to find the 2016 Personal Year Number for birth date December 11th, 1969, the calculation would be:

1+2+1+1+2+0+1+6 = 14

1+4 = **5 Personal Year Number**

Personal Year Number 1

New Beginnings, Action, Opportunity

The 1 Personal Year follows directly after the 9 Personal Year of "endings and completion", and so it represents new beginnings and creating a fresh start. This year, you can wipe the slate clean and begin a brand new nine-year cycle aimed toward improving yourself and your overall quality of life. Everything you do this year (and the attitude you take while doing it) will set the tone for the following nine years, so it's vital that you maintain a positive mindset and be proactive about making improvements.

Big changes and new opportunities will present themselves this year, so don't procrastinate or you may miss the boat. The masculine energy of Number 1 will encourage you to be decisive and take action, and you'll experience an influx of renewed energy and new ideas. It's important that you give these ideas sufficient time to marinate and grow for they could take the entire 12 months to come to fruition. Whatever you do, don't give up if they don't happen straight away. Be proactive yet patient at the same time. Meditate regularly to enhance your intuition. That way you'll know which logical steps to take and you'll be able to distinguish the good ideas from time-wasters.

This is a year in which to be courageous and to make decisions that reflect your true, authentic self as opposed to compromising your needs to conform to society or to please others. Be the real you. For the next 12 months you must learn to focus on yourself and put your own needs first (within reason). Whether it's getting a makeover, focusing on self-improvement, or taking steps toward making your life the way you want it to be - this year is all about *you*.

This is a year in which to:

- Get in the driver's seat of your life and move forward
- Be proactive and take action
- Begin something new such as a relationship, a career, a project, a hobby etc. ...
- Develop and implement new ideas
- Start a healthier lifestyle
- Focus on self-improvement
- Be independent and self-reliant
- Increase your self-confidence
- Be your true, authentic self
- Plan your goals for the next nine years
- Stay positive and have a fresh approach
- Be open to new opportunities
- Manifest your dreams into reality
- Take on a leadership role

Michelle's manifestation tip

Number 1 is a "creative" number so this is a very powerful manifestation cycle for turning your dreams into reality, or at the very least to set things up for future manifestation. This year it pays to familiarize yourself with the Law of Attraction and the work of Abraham-Hicks,* so you can use it to your advantage. Number 1

* Abraham-Hicks are world leaders in Law of Attraction teachings. You can visit their website for further information: www.abraham-hicks.com

rules the mind, therefore consistent creative visualization and a positive mindset can increase your chance of success. Work out what you want, focus all of your energy upon it, and follow through with practical action.

Affirmation

"I am open to new beginnings that improve my quality of life."

Personal Year Number 2

Patience, Relationships, Balance, Emotions

Where last year's 1 Personal Year was about being proactive and taking action, the 2 Personal Year is about stabilizing and consolidating what you've already created and waiting for things to come to you. As this is a slow-paced year, there will be times when you'll feel as if nothing is happening at all. But don't be fooled by this lack of activity, as things are still happening "behind the scenes." If there's one thing that will guarantee your success in a slow moving 2 Year, it's patience.

Should things happen to come to standstill - don't panic. It's simply the Universe giving last year's changes and improvements the time they need to solidify and mature. In the meantime live in the present moment and take advantage of calming/grounding practices such as yoga, meditation, or qi gong to maintain balance and a positive mindset. Listening, singing, writing, or playing music you love during this time is extremely beneficial, too.

Love, relationships, emotions, and matters of the heart come to the forefront this year. Existing relationships will be challenged or get stronger and those who are single may meet someone special (or several special people). Either way, life is giving you a chance to explore your emotional side in a 2 Year and that can manifest itself in many different ways - each person's experience is different. However, common events in a 2 Year include: heartfelt love; meeting a soul mate; heartache, loss, or disappointment; repressed emotions coming to the surface; a deeper connection to others; happiness and joy.

This is also a year in which to focus on self-love and developing a strong relationship with yourself. Be kind to yourself and surround yourself with good people. Strive to create balance in every area of your life. Be cooperative, compromise, and seek harmony in all that you do. You're going to feel hypersensitive this year, so try not to blow things out of proportion. However, with this heightened sensitivity come increased intuition and extrasensory experiences. So take advantage of this by following your gut feeling at all times, as well as developing your psychic abilities, if you feel that way inclined.

This is a year in which to:

- Consolidate and solidify what you started last year
- Build upon what you already have
- Be patient and wait for opportunities to come to you
- Practice mindfulness; take up meditation, yoga, or qi gong
- Focus on your health and wellbeing

- Recognize, express, and release repressed emotions
- Work on self-love
- Develop psychic abilities and enhance your intuition
- Work on personal development
- Be positive and proactive about finding love
- Improve your existing relationships with others

Michelle's manifestation tip

In order to manifest your dreams in a 2 Year you need to get clear about what you want and fine-tune the details "behind the scenes" as opposed to taking action and forcing things to happen. You must trust in the Universe's plan and allow things to unfold in Divine order and timing. Remember at all times that "what is meant for you won't pass you by" as you trust your intuition to guide you toward the next logical step. Take advantage of your heightened sensitivity by tapping into the emotion of what it would "feel" like to have your desire in your life. And visualize it for at least 15 minutes a day.

Affirmation

"I am emotionally balanced and open to giving and receiving love."

Personal Year Number 3

Socialization, Self-expression, Communication, Creativity

Where there were delays and frustrations last year, things speed back up again in the 3 Personal Year. It's full steam ahead as the things you created in your 1 Year begin to pay off and take flight. This is a year in which you finally start to reap what you've sown. There is a lot going on, so extra effort is required in terms of planning, discipline, and focus. If you scatter your energy in too many directions or have your finger in too many pies, things can easily spiral out of control and you may not accomplish anything. Being organized and grounded is the key to your success.

The 3 Year is a year in which to be social and to spend time with others, so reconnect with old friends and be open to making new friends. Your social calendar will liven up, so you may feel a desire to entertain as well as to attend gatherings and events. Due to your heightened personal expression at this time, you may find you develop the gift of the gab or a need to express your thoughts and feelings. It doesn't matter whether you do this through conversation, journaling, writing an email, poem, blog, or song, as long as you speak your truth and communicate what you feel. This is also a year of enhanced creativity, so if you have a creative project you'd like to work on, now is the time to do it.

This is typically an upbeat year with "fun" and "joy" being the dominant themes, so it's important to do more of what you enjoy. Whether it's taking a vacation, gardening, cooking, dancing, listening to music, or spending time on a hobby - if it makes you feel good - do more of it! Number 3 amplifies the emotions, so it's important that you have an optimistic attitude throughout the year and see the glass half full at all times because your attitude will determine how this year unfolds. Avoid gossiping and complaining, and monitor your budget, as 3 encourages spending.

This is a year in which to:

- Be social and connect with others
- Entertain family and friends
- Attend gatherings and events
- Have fun and do more of what you enjoy
- Be creative - perhaps by working on a new project
- Write a blog, a memoir, a poem, or a book
- Start journaling
- Take up a hobby
- Travel or go on vacation
- Be optimistic and see the glass half full
- Monitor your spending
- Express yourself honestly
- Communicate your thoughts and feelings

Michelle's manifestation tip

In order to manifest your goals and dreams you need to maintain a "high vibration." Your vibration is governed by your emotions and one of the most powerful ways to raise it is to do more of what you enjoy. In other words, you just need to do more of what makes you feel good, and less of what doesn't make you feel good. It's really as simple as that. This is a year of happiness and joy when it's easier for you to tap into your positive emotions. So be optimistic, laugh more, and make time for fun – this will help you attract the things you want with greater ease.

Affirmation

"I am optimistic and happy, and I live a joyful life."

Personal Year Number 4

Order, Effort, Building, Planning

The 4 Personal Year is all about doing whatever needs to be done to make your life the best it can be. It's about knuckling down, being organized, and putting systems in place that enable things to flow more smoothly. This may involve getting fit and healthy, studying something that will increase your earning potential, setting up insurance, doing maintenance on your home, emptying out the attic, or getting on top of your paperwork. It will involve a variety of personal and work-related chores that will benefit you in the long run, providing you put the effort in.

This is a year in which to plan your future goals and to take steps toward achieving them. For the next 12 months, life is giving you an opportunity to build a firm foundation for your future, so don't waste it. You can have some great accomplishments this year and make major headway; however, your attitude is the key to your success. There may be obstacles, frustrations, and delays, but with patience and perseverance, you'll get there in the end. Your dedication and determination will be tested this year, so don't give up when the going gets tough. Just pick yourself up and soldier on.

You'll be more focused than last year, so prioritize your time, work on the details behind the scenes, and finish what you start. This is also a year in which to put down some roots and commit to your future; therefore it's a good time to save money, pay off debts, solidify your relationships, start a family, and buy a business or a home. Regardless of what you do, it's about making long-term decisions that make things more secure. Be sensible and practical, as this isn't a year in which to be adventurous or take risks. Extra physical, mental, and emotional effort is required of you, but with effort come rewards. Providing you have a positive mindset, this will be an extremely significant year.

This is a year in which to:

- Work hard
- Build a solid foundation
- Plan your future and take action
- Get organized, put systems in place
- Budget and save money
- Pay off debts
- Focus on your mental and physical health
- Make a commitment
- Study
- Buy a business or a home
- Start a family
- Make time to relax and unwind

Michelle's manifestation tip

This is a year when "practical action" is required to manifest your goals and dreams. But how do you determine what is the right action to take when you're unsure or faced with a variety of options?

Firstly, you need to get in alignment with the Universe so you can receive clear and accurate guidance as to the right direction to take. This is called "Inspired Action" and it comes from Source (God, the Universe, the Divine). Your higher self knows the next logical step to take and the Universe will guide you, but the more you quieten down your mind, the clearer the message you receive will be. Use meditation, which is a very powerful tool to help still the mind.

Affirmation

"I am physically, emotionally, mentally, and financially secure."

Personal Year Number 5

Adventure, Progress, Movement, Change

After last year's effort and hard work, you've now entered a dynamic and action-packed year full of both expected and unexpected change. Because the 5 Personal Year is midway between the 1 Personal Year of "new beginnings" and the 9 Personal Year of "endings," life decides to shake things up by creating necessary changes, whether you're prepared for them or not. Therefore, it pays to be flexible and adaptable and be ready to go with the flow. That way you can roll with whatever comes your way.

Change is inevitable and can manifest in many forms. For some it could be a change in location, residence, relationship, or job, and for others it may be a change in attitude, direction, or lifestyle. Either way, there'll be many options to choose from, so break away from old routines and launch yourself into new areas of challenge and growth. You may experience feelings of restlessness and boredom, or simply being "stuck" - but don't make hasty decisions. Think before you act.

This year can trigger a desire to overindulge your senses with food, alcohol, overspending, or sex. So don't go off the rails or throw caution to the wind. Discipline and moderation are the keys to your success. This is an exciting year when it pays to promote yourself and to network with others. Travel, exploration, and adventure lie at your fingertips, so get out and about and try new things. However, try not to scatter your energy in too many directions as things could spiral out of control. The 5 Year can either be exhilarating or challenging, depending on your mindset.

This is a year in which to:

- Make changes and prepare for change
- Be fun and adventurous
- Create more personal freedom
- Experience new things
- Take a vacation
- Travel nationally and/or internationally
- Move house, town, or country
- Advertise and promote yourself
- Be social, network with others
- Change job or career
- Take a calculated risk

Michelle's manifestation tip

This is a year in which to believe in "miracles and magic" in order to attract them into your life. Anything can happen in a 5 Year, so dare to believe in your dreams. Be optimistic and expect surprises and lucky breaks. Look back on your life for evidence of lucky breaks in your past and believe that they can happen again. This is a year of opportunity, but you must learn to recognize the opportunities when they arise. Make an effort to seize any kind of opportunity regardless of how big or small it may be. Since you attract what you think about the most, when you think mainly about opportunities, magic, and miracles, you will attract these into your life.

Affirmation

"I make positive and exciting changes that improve my quality of life."

Personal Year Number 6

Love, Family, Domestic Responsibility

The 6 Personal Year is one in which to be of service to others and to attend to your responsibilities. It may involve an element of sacrifice, so prepare to put others' needs before your own. There's a big difference between helping others because you "have to" and helping others because you "want to," and this year will reflect that. For the next 12 months your loved ones and family come first, so try to serve them willingly.

This is the perfect time to mend broken relationships and to touch base with family members you haven't spoken to in a while. It's also a year when you dedicate extra time to your children, grandchildren, or other children within the family. You may become a shoulder to cry on, so offer your assistance where you can. Whether it's taking care of elderly relatives, nursing a sick family member or friend, or babysitting your nephew, it's natural to experience feelings of martyrdom and resentment. However, it's important to process these feelings in a healthy way and to remember "it isn't going to be forever."

Number 6 governs love, marriage, separation, and divorce - and some people will experience these things in a 6 Year. Others will experience the 6 energy in different ways such as engaging in a community project, having a child, working in a service-based career, or starting a home-based business (as this is a favorable time to do so). The 6 Year is a good time for singles to find love and for existing relationships to move to a deeper level of understanding and commitment. For others, relationship issues that have been brewing beneath the surface will rise to be resolved and unstable relationships may end. Either way, this is a year in which to ensure that the relationships in your life are the best that they can be.

If you'd like to spend some extra time in the garden or do some much-needed work on your property, this is the year to do so. Renovating, redecorating, or rearranging may do your home the world of good. This is a good year for career advancement, especially for those in a service-based career. Number 6 represents beauty and physical appearance, so a makeover, a new wardrobe, or a change in hairstyle may boost your self-esteem. Other things to focus on this year are self-love, health, and the healing or creative arts.

This is a year in which to:

- Take your responsibilities seriously
- Be there for family and friends
- Be of service to others
- Focus on domestic affairs
- Renovate or redecorate your home
- Be creative – take up a new hobby
- Work on your garden
- Start a home-based business
- Get married
- Start a family
- Get a makeover
- Engage in a community project

Michelle's manifestation tip

Number 6 is the number of "love" and love is the key to manifesting your dreams this year. In order to attract the things you want, you must maintain a high vibration and you can help do this by choosing to see the world through the eyes of love, which will automatically raise your vibration. When you look beyond the illusion to see the beauty in the world, you align yourself with Source and improve your quality of life. Unconditional self-love, along with love and appreciation for life, is the key to your success this year. Being of service and feeling love and compassion toward others will bring you closer to your dreams.

Affirmation

"I joyfully serve others and enhance my own life in return."

Personal Year Number 7

Introspection, Personal and Spiritual Growth

Where last year you focused on serving others, this year the focus is on building a better relationship with yourself. The 7 Personal Year encourages self-analysis, so that you form a deeper understanding of who you are, what you want, and why you're here. Your main agenda over the next 12 months is personal development, spiritual wisdom, and going within to find the answers you seek. This isn't a time to chase new opportunities or to conquer the business world. Instead, it's a time to take a step back and reflect. This is a very important year when the more inner work you do, the greater your success in the outer world - in your 8 Personal Year, next year.

Your capacity for research and understanding is at its peak, so it's a favorable year to study or to develop an existing skill - especially anything that is related to IT and computers, science, psychology, engineering, analytics, metaphysics, philosophy, and conventional or alternative health. If you wish to become a specialist in your craft, this is the year to do it. This is also a year in which to focus on spirituality, spend time in nature, and contemplate the meaning of life. Your intuition is at an all-time high, so follow your inner guidance at all times.

If you suffered a loss or heartbreak last year, use this year to process and heal. Explore alternative therapies if you feel that way inclined. Don't force things to happen this year, wait for things to come to you, as opportunities will present themselves next year. In the meantime, get a health check, exercise, take up a spiritual practice such as yoga, meditation, EFT (Tapping), Reiki, or qi gong, and enhance your connection to Source (Universe, God, Divine). Build a strong inner foundation in preparation for the years to come. In fact, your future success depends upon the positive changes you make today.

This is a year in which to:

- Adopt a spiritual practice
- Spend quiet time alone
- Take up meditation, yoga, EFT, or qi gong
- Explore alternative therapies
- Detox and eat a healthy diet
- Spend time in nature
- Rest, recuperate, and relax
- Focus on personal development
- Study or become a specialist
- Go on a spiritual retreat, expand your spiritual learning
- Get closer to God
- Improve your health, get a health check, exercise

Michelle's manifestation tip

Getting back to basics is the key to manifesting your dreams this year. In order to manifest your dreams you need to maintain a high vibration, and one of the best ways to do that is to spend more time in nature. Allow nature to re-energize and replenish you as you meditate on the land with the intention of connecting with the healing power of Mother Earth. Give thanks and appreciation for the beauty around you and visualize the Universe beaming you up with golden white light and love. By spending more time alone, improving yourself from within, and getting closer to God (Source, the Universe, the Divine), you'll manifest your dreams with greater ease.

Affirmation

"As I improve myself, I improve the circumstances of my life."

Personal Year Number 8

Manifestation, Personal Power, Finances, Career

The 8 Personal Year focuses on business, career, property, finances, and legal matters. For some there will be opportunities for career advancement, recognition, and financial gain, while others may experience an increase in expenses or financial loss. Either way, 8 is the number of karmic balance that rebalances the scales of justice in direct proportion to your attitude and actions of the past – especially since your 1 Personal Year. You'll reap what you've sown in an 8 year, and whatever you began in your 1 Year will now begin to pay off. If you've been honest and hardworking, you'll be rewarded in some way, either financially, through recognition, or by attracting favorable opportunities.

This year is all about balance – especially balancing the material and spiritual worlds. On the one hand you're being encouraged to have a positive relationship with money and to adopt an attitude of abundance, yet on the other you cannot allow yourself to become consumed by the accumulation of money and material goods, power, status, or success. You need to obtain balance and find the middle ground in between. Wherever you are out of balance in your life, the 8 Year will point it out, giving you the opportunity to re-adjust.

The 8 Year will also encourage you to reclaim your personal power over anything or anyone that has caused you to feel disempowered in some way. Whether it's an overpowering person, an addiction, a fear, or a belief, this is the year to assert yourself, confront it once and for all, and take ownership of your power. On the other hand, you must be mindful not to overpower or disempower others.

In addition, the Number 8 Year represents money and manifestation, so get your finances in order and be mindful not to overspend. This is a powerful cycle of manifestation when you can attract what you focus on, so focus on the positives and minimize your fears. This is a very karmic year in which major lessons will be learned, and important connections will be made. Significant people, who can enhance your career or your overall quality of life, will cross your path. Since 8 governs the Law of Cause and Effect, it's essential that you watch your motivations behind everything you do, and live with honesty and integrity at all times.

This is a year in which to:

- Budget, save money, get your finances in order
- Deal with outstanding legal matters
- Work hard, be honest and ethical
- Build your career
- Study something that advances your career
- Apply for a promotion
- Start a new job or career
- Reclaim your personal power
- Familiarize yourself with the Law of Attraction
- Manifest your goals and dreams
- Adopt an attitude of abundance
- Reprogram your limiting beliefs

Michelle's manifestation tip

This is a year in which to put your goals and dreams at the forefront of your mind. As 8 is the number of manifestation, this is one of the most powerful cycles to manifest your dreams. Because you attract what you think about *the most*, this year you need to think *mostly* about what you want. One of most effective tools that enables you do this is a vision board.

To create a vision board, gather images, words, and positive affirmations that represent your dreams and activate a positive emotional response within you. Glue them onto a notice board or a large piece of cardboard and put it somewhere where you'll see it throughout the day. View your vision board as often as you can.

Visualize and meditate upon the images and imagine your dreams coming true. This will activate their vibration and help attract them into your life.

Affirmation

"The Universe is abundant and I am financially safe and secure."

Personal Year Number 9

Transformation, Completion, Endings

This is the final year of your nine-year cycle, and it focuses on completion and transformation in preparation for new beginnings. A major part of this transformation involves letting go of the things in your life that no longer serve you – whether it's a job, a friendship, a relationship, a residence, a mind-set, or behavior you may have outgrown. Either way, this is a time to spring-clean your life so you can move toward better things.

To make the most of this year, trust in the Divine plan; surrender to change; forgive others and yourself; and accept, let go, and move on when things don't go your way. Despite this being a year of endings, it's also a year of rebirth and compensation, when everything you've been striving for can finally come to fruition. In other words, this is your pay-off year – so start feeling deserving and worthy. Expect the best and you'll get the best, especially this year.

The 9 Year encourages you to focus on being of service and following humanitarian pursuits by donating your time, money, attention, or unwanted items to a good cause. Perhaps you could do something to assist the environment or offer a helping hand to a charity, a person, a family, or an animal in need. Compassion and forgiveness play a major role this year, so be open-minded toward others and resolve outstanding conflicts and disputes.

This is a year in which to:

- Spring-clean your life and home
- Let go of bad habits
- Move house
- Leave an unfulfilling job
- Tie up loose ends
- End an unhealthy relationship
- Clean out your closets
- Donate to charity
- Work for a cause
- Forgive others and the past
- Resolve outstanding conflicts
- Heal outstanding emotional wounds

Michelle's manifestation tip

This is a year to let go, trust, and surrender in order to manifest your dreams. Desperation prevents manifestation; so the more you struggle to attract your desire, the more you push it away. In order to attract what you want, you must give the Universe space to deliver your request. This can only be achieved by getting out of the way so that everything can unfold as it should. It isn't your job to *make* it happen; it is simply your job to *let* it happen. When you surrender the outcome to the Divine, you let the magic flow. Make peace with your life as it is today, and appreciate what you already have, so you can make your dreams come true.

Affirmation

"It is safe to surrender to the magical future that awaits me."

Personal Month Numbers and Their Meanings

Now, let's take a look at the Personal Month Number.

Whereas your Personal Year Number reveals your forecast for the year, your Personal Month Number reveals your forecast for each of the 12 months within the year. Even though your Personal Year Number has the greatest influence over your life, it pays to know your Personal Month Number for each month to gain a broader understanding of the conditions and opportunities around you.

Interesting fact

The key to an accurate forecast lies in blending your Personal Year and Personal Month Number forecasts together, then using your intuition and common sense to evaluate what this combination could mean. For example, in a 9 Personal Year of endings, August is an 8 Personal Month that focuses on finances and career. When you blend them together, this could indicate a change in your financial situation or changes in the workplace. It could also mean the end of a particular duty within your job – or even a promotion! The possibilities are endless.

How to calculate your Personal Month Number

Step 1: Add your *Personal Year Number* to the calendar month you're enquiring about.

Step 2: Add any double-digit numbers together to get a single-digit *Personal Month Number* between 1 and 9.

For example, to find the Personal Month Number for June if you're in a 5 Personal Year, the calculation would be:

5 (Personal Year Number)
+ 6 (Calendar Month Number for June) = 11
1+1 = **2 Personal Month Number**

Therefore June is a 2 Personal Month in a 5 Personal Year.

The following table shows Calendar Month Numbers to get you started.

Calendar Month Numbers

January = 1	May = 5	September = 9
February = 2	June = 6	October = 1
March = 3	July = 7	November = 2
April = 4	August = 8	December = 3

Personal Month Number 1

New Beginnings, Action, Opportunity

This is a month in which to take action and begin new things. New opportunities will present themselves, so don't be afraid to take them. This is also a good time to be ambitious, determined, and decisive – to get in the driver's seat of your life and take charge. Have the courage to make changes, break new ground, and try new things.

Personal Month Number 2

Patience, Relationships, Balance, Emotions

This is a month when it's good to step back and be patient. Don't force things to happen. Obtain stability in what you've already created and work on the finer details behind the scenes. Seek balance, peace, and harmony in your relationships and be cooperative with others. Heal your past hurts, express your emotions in a healthy way, and be open to giving and receiving love.

Personal Month Number 3

Socialization, Self-expression, Communication, Creativity

This is a month in which to add more happiness into your life and to do more of what brings you joy. Be social, spend time with friends, have fun, and dabble in creative endeavors. Regardless of what is going on in your life, it is important that you maintain an optimistic attitude. This is also the time to express yourself and to communicate your thoughts and feelings honestly.

Personal Month Number 4

Order, Effort, Building, Planning

This is a month when it's good to get your business and personal life in order. Be organized, focused, and proactive - and complete any unfinished projects. This is a time to work hard and put effort into every area of your life, because with effort come rewards. Create stability and build a strong foundation. Plan ahead - don't procrastinate or waste time. Persevere through challenges and don't give up.

Personal Month Number 5

Adventure, Progress, Movement, Change

This is a month when it's good to step out of your comfort zone - to be adventurous and try new things. Be flexible and adaptable and prepare yourself for change. If there are changes you need to make in your life, now is the time to make them. This is a dynamic and fast-paced month so focus and prioritize your time, and don't have your finger in too many pies. Be social and promote yourself.

Personal Month Number 6

Love, Family, Domestic Responsibility

This is a month in which to be responsible and fulfill your obligations - especially relating to your home, relationships, and family. Make time for those who need your assistance, attention, or time, and spend quality time with your children. Unresolved issues with others will rise to be addressed. This is a time to improve your relationships and focus on giving and receiving love.

Personal Month Number 7

Rest, Introspection, Personal and Spiritual Growth

This is a month when it's good to take a step back from the hustle and bustle of life to recharge your batteries. Spend quiet time alone to contemplate your life purpose and how you can improve your life. This is a time to get in touch with your spiritual side and to focus on becoming a better person. Work on improving your health and explore alternative modalities such as yoga and meditation.

Personal Month Number 8

Manifestation, Personal Power, Finances, Career

This is a month in which to budget and get your finances in order. Work hard and don't overspend. A career opportunity may present itself or there may be chance to attract or spend money. This is a favorable time to make career changes. Be ambitious, stand up for yourself, and take action. Adopt an attitude of abundance and be positive, because 8 is the number of manifestation.

Personal Month Number 9

Transformation, Completion, Endings

This is a month of endings and transformation, so it's time to let go of the old to make way for the new. Let go of bad habits, people, and anything you no longer need in your life. Don't be afraid for things to come to an end, because better opportunities await. This is also a month in which to be of service to others - to volunteer your money, assistance, or time to a good cause or someone in need. Forgive the misfortune in your life and move on.

Personal Year and Personal Month Number Combinations

As the key to an accurate forecast lies in combining your Personal Year and Personal Month Number forecasts together, here are some handy Personal Year and Personal Month Combination Forecasts to make it a little easier for you.

Personal Year 1 - Personal Months

New Beginnings, Action, Opportunity

January

In this 1 Year of new beginnings, action, and opportunity, January is a 2 Personal Month. You'll be eager to move forward but your patience is required for a little longer. This is a month in which to release repressed emotions and obtain emotional balance. Singles could meet someone special, so be open to giving and receiving love.

February

In this 1 Year of new beginnings, action, and opportunity, February is a 3 Personal Month. Things begin to speed up now and you're feeling optimistic and social. This is a favorable time to pursue creative projects and express your thoughts and feelings to others.

March

In this 1 Year of new beginnings, action, and opportunity, March is a 4 Personal Month. This is a month in which to be focused and disciplined, and to work hard. You're going to be busy, so prioritize your time, take care of details, and persevere through challenges.

April

In this 1 Year of new beginnings, action, and opportunity, April is a 5 Personal Month. This is a fast-moving month full of surprises and change. If there are changes you need to make in your life, now is the time to make them. This is a favorable period in which to advertise and promote yourself.

May

In this 1 Year of new beginnings, action, and opportunity, May is a 6 Personal Month. This is month in which to focus on your relationships and family. It is a favorable time to renovate or create a new environment within an existing home. New romance can bloom under this vibration.

June

In this 1 Year of new beginnings, action, and opportunity, June is a 7 Personal Month. This is a slow-moving month so don't force things to happen. Instead, go within to regroup and re-evaluate your master plan. This is a time to meditate and reconnect with your spiritual side.

July

In this 1 Year of new beginnings, action, and opportunity, July is an 8 Personal Month. This is a time when business, career, and finances take center stage. Be mindful not to overspend, and use your money wisely. A new business opportunity may present itself.

August

In this 1 Year of new beginnings, action, and opportunity, August is a 9 Personal Month. Life is giving you an opportunity to let go of what no longer serves you, so you can move forward with a clean slate. Don't hold on to what you've outgrown, as better things await.

September

In this 1 Year of new beginnings, action, and opportunity, September is a 1 Personal Month. It's full steam ahead this month, so be on the lookout for new opportunities and seize them with confidence. Be ambitious and move forward with courage.

October

In this 1 Year of new beginnings, action, and opportunity, October is a 2 Personal Month. For the second time this year you're being encouraged to slow down and take a step back to focus on your relationships and your emotions. This is a favorable time for singles to find love.

November

In this 1 Year of new beginnings, action, and opportunity, November is a 3 Personal Month. This a month in which to get out and about and have some fun, but be mindful of overindulgence. Be responsible. Discipline and focus are the keys to your success this month.

December

In this 1 Year of new beginnings, action, and opportunity, December is a 4 Personal Month. You'll need to work hard right up until the end of the year, but with effort come rewards. Get everything in order so you can take a well-earned rest over the holidays.

Personal Year 2 – Personal Months

Patience, Relationships, Balance, Emotions

January

In this 2 Year that focuses on patience, relationships, balance, and emotions, January is a 3 Personal Month. This is an upbeat month in which to be social and have some fun. It's also a great time for a vacation. The numbers 2 and 3 amplify the emotions, so don't blow things out of proportion.

February

In this 2 Year that focuses on patience, relationships, balance, and emotions, February is a 4 Personal Month. This is a time to get organized and work on details behind the scenes to ensure everything in your life runs smoothly.

Your workload will increase, so put time aside to rest and re-energize.

March

In this 2 Year that focuses on patience, relationships, balance, and emotions, March is a 5 Personal Month. Prepare for random events and unexpected changes. If you're single, be adventurous. Step out of your comfort zone to try new things. Promote yourself and your work.

April

In this 2 Year that focuses on patience, relationships, balance, and emotions, April is a 6 Personal Month. This is a time to focus on your relationships and matters of the heart. Relationship issues with loved ones and family will surface to be addressed. Be honest about your feelings.

May

In this 2 Year that focuses on patience, relationships, balance, and emotions, May is a 7 Personal Month. You're extremely intuitive this month, so follow your gut instincts at all times. It's a good time to have a reading or healing, or to explore alternative modalities.

June

In this 2 Year that focuses on patience, relationships, balance, and emotions, June is an 8 Personal Month. Business and money matters come to the forefront. Put extra effort in at work and assert yourself. Be ambitious yet diplomatic and cooperative at the same time.

July

In this 2 Year that focuses on patience, relationships, balance, and emotions, July is a 9 Personal Month. Relationships that are hanging on by a thread will come up for review this month. Let go of anything that isn't good for you or anyone in your life who prevents you from being happy.

August

In this 2 Year that focuses on patience, relationships, balance, and emotions, August is a 1 Personal Month. You feel re-energized and revitalized and ready to conquer new things. Be on the lookout for new and exciting opportunities, especially when it comes to romance.

September

In this 2 Year that focuses on patience, relationships, balance, and emotions, September is a 2 Personal Month. You are highly sensitive and intuitive, so use this to your advantage. Meditation and quiet time alone will help you decipher intuitive hints and insights. Be kind to yourself and do things to nurture your spirit.

October

In this 2 Year that focuses on patience, relationships, balance, and emotions, October is a 3 Personal Month. Things begin to speed up now and you're optimistic and adventurous. Do something fun, be social, start a new hobby, or attend an event. Spend time with friends.

November

In this 2 Year that focuses on patience, relationships, balance, and emotions, November is a 4 Personal Month. This is a month in which to tidy up loose ends and do what needs to be done. Extra physical, mental, and emotional effort is required this month, so give it your all.

December

In this 2 Year that focuses on patience, relationships, balance, and emotions, December is a 5 Personal Month. This is a dynamic and fast-moving month with a lot going on. Changes will present themselves, so be adaptable and go with the flow. Travel or take a vacation if you can.

Personal Year 3 - Personal Months

Socialization, Self-expression, Communication, Creativity

January

In this 3 Year that focuses on socialization, self-expression, communication, and creativity, January is a 4 Personal Month. This is a time to knuckle down and do some work. You're easily distracted this month, so extra effort is required to focus on the job at hand. Be mindful not to overspend.

February

In this 3 Year that focuses on socialization, self-expression, communication, and creativity, February is a 5 Personal Month. This is a dynamic and fast-paced month when anything can happen - and usually does. Be flexible, adaptable, and go with the flow. Communication flows easily. Promote yourself.

March

In this 3 Year that focuses on socialization, self-expression, communication, and creativity, March is a 6 Personal Month. This is a favorable time for singles to find love so get off the couch and mingle. Be a helping hand or a shoulder to cry on for those in need. Have fun but be responsible.

April

In this 3 Year that focuses on socialization, self-expression, communication, and creativity, April is a 7 Personal Month. This is a time to ask the big questions, "What do I want from my life?" and "What do I need to do to get it?" Focus on your personal and spiritual development.

May

In this 3 Year that focuses on socialization, self-expression, communication, and creativity, May is an 8 Personal Month. This is a favorable time for business and career opportunities, so be ambitious, positive, and proactive. Think and believe you're lucky.

June

In this 3 Year that focuses on socialization, self-expression, communication, and creativity, June is a 9 Personal Month. When one door closes, another door opens, so have the courage to walk through it. Let go of anyone or anything that prevents you from being happy.

July

In this 3 Year that focuses on socialization, self-expression, communication, and creativity, July is a 1 Personal Month. You feel energized and ready to conquer new projects and opportunities. Now is the time to move forward. Don't be hesitant or indecisive. It's full steam ahead.

August

In this 3 Year that focuses on socialization, self-expression, communication, and creativity, August is a 2 Personal Month. You're going to feel hypersensitive this month, so try not to overreact or take things too personally. This is a favorable time for singles to find love.

September

In this 3 Year that focuses on socialization, self-expression, communication and creativity, September is a 3 Personal Month. This is a month in which to be creative and joyful. Take a vacation, socialize, and do something fun. Express your thoughts and feeling with others honestly.

October

In this 3 Year that focuses on socialization, self-expression, communication, and creativity, October is a 4 Personal Month. You may face obstacles and delays but rewards are there for the taking. Be proactive, focused, and disciplined. Persevere to achieve your goals.

November

In this 3 Year that focuses on socialization, self-expression, communication, and creativity, November is a 5 Personal

Month. This is a time to be adventurous and to take a chance. Make changes and try new things. Promote yourself. Be organized and prioritize your time.

December

In this 3 Year that focuses on socialization, self-expression, communication, and creativity, December is a 6 Personal Month. This is a time to forgive those who have upset you in the past. Be there for loved ones, neighbors, family and friends.

Personal Year 4 – Personal Months

Order, Effort, Building, Planning

January

In this 4 Year that focuses on order, effort, building, and planning, January is a 5 Personal Month. There's a lot going on so you may find it hard to stabilize and focus. Organization is the key. This is a time to advertise, network, and promote. Change is unavoidable, so go with the flow.

February

In this 4 Year that focuses on order, effort, building, and planning, February is a 6 Personal Month. This is a time to focus on domestic, relationship, and family matters. It's a favorable time to buy, sell, repair, redecorate, or renovate a home. Be there for family and others in need.

March

In this 4 Year that focuses on order, effort, building, and planning, March is a 7 Personal Month. This is a time to focus your attention inward to contemplate your master plan for the next ten months. Identify what's holding you back and work toward overcoming these obstacles.

April

In this 4 year that focuses on order, effort, building, and planning, April is an 8 Personal Month. Dedicate this month to your financial, legal, and business affairs. Be organized, get everything in order, budget your finances, deal with outstanding matters and work hard to reap rewards.

May

In this 4 Year that focuses on order, effort, building, and planning, May is a 9 Personal Month. This is a time to finish ongoing projects and tie up loose ends. It's out with the old to make way for the new, so look for opportunities to make a positive change. Be optimistic about your future.

June

In this 4 Year that focuses on order, effort, building, and planning, June is a 1 Personal Month. New opportunities will cross your path so be proactive and seize the moment. Don't procrastinate or hold back out of fear of the unknown. Be courageous and take a chance.

July

In this 4 Year that focuses on order, effort, building, and planning, July is a 2 Personal Month. This is a time to concentrate on the relationships in your life: both work-related and personal. Be diplomatic and cooperative in order to get the outcome you desire. Singles may find love.

August

In this 4 Year that focuses on order, effort, building, and planning, August is a 3 Personal Month. This is a time to unwind and take a vacation if you can. It may be hard to concentrate at work, so be extra disciplined and focused to get things done. Make time to socialize and have fun.

September

In this 4 Year that focuses on order, effort, building, and planning, September is a 4 Personal Month. Should you experience obstacles and delays remember, "This too shall pass." Don't let your challenges hinder your desire to succeed. Your persistence will pay off.

October

In this 4 Year that focuses on order, effort, building, and planning, October is a 5 Personal Month. This is a time of both expected and unexpected developments. If changes need to be made to improve your personal life and/or career, this is the month in which to make them.

November

In this 4 Year that focuses on order, effort, building, and planning, November is a 6 Personal Month. Issues that have been building up with work colleagues, loved ones, family members, or friends will rise to be addressed. Make your relationships the best they can be.

December

In this 4 Year that focuses on order, effort, building, and planning, December is a 7 Personal Month. This is a month in which to analyze and strategize your future goals and how they can be achieved. Take time out for well-deserved rest, as relaxation is essential. Spend quiet time alone.

Personal Year 5 – Personal Months

Adventure, Progress, Movement, Change

January

In this 5 Year that focuses on adventure, progress, movement, and change, January is a 6 Personal Month. This month could bring expected or unexpected changes to family, relationships, domestic affairs, or the home. Offer a helping hand or listen sympathetically to those in need.

February

In this 5 Year that focuses on adventure, progress, movement, and change, February is a 7 Personal Month. This is a time to stabilize yourself from within so you can weather the changes ahead. Focus on your health and wellbeing and take up meditation if you haven't already.

March

In this 5 Year that focuses on adventure, progress, movement, and change, March is an 8 Personal Month. Make necessary changes to improve your finances and career. Be ambitious, promote yourself, and adopt an attitude of abundance. Believe in your dreams.

April

In this 5 Year that focuses on adventure, progress, movement, and change, April is a 9 Personal Month. This is a time of endings and completion, so spring-clean your home and your life. Eliminate unhealthy habits. Forgive your misfortunes of the past and move on to better things.

May

In this 5 Year that focuses on adventure, progress, movement, and change, May is a 1 Personal Month. This is a very progressive and fast-moving month when new opportunities will present themselves in your personal life and career. Seize the moment. Be confident and take a leap of faith.

June

In this 5 Year that focuses on adventure, progress, movement, and change, June is a 2 Personal Month. This is a time to work on your emotional side and your relationships with others. Be diplomatic, as issues that have been brewing beneath the surface will rise to be addressed.

July

In this 5 Year that focuses on adventure, progress, movement, and change, July is a 3 Personal Month. This is a dynamic and action-packed month with a lot going on. Focus and discipline are essential, as is prioritizing your time. Be social, take a vacation, and have some fun.

August

In this 5 year that focuses on adventure, progress, movement, and change, August is a 4 Personal Month. This is a time to get organized and to make sure everything in your personal life and career are in order. Put in extra effort this month and be prepared to work hard - with effort comes reward.

September

In this 5 Year that focuses on adventure, progress, movement, and change, September is a 5 Personal Month. This is a time to get out and about, and to promote yourself. Be mindful of the temptation to misbehave or to overindulge in physical pleasures - moderation is the key. Expect a surprise.

October

In this 5 Year that focuses on adventure, progress, movement, and change, October is a 6 Personal Month. You may be a shoulder to cry on for your partner, a family member, or a friend. Relationships, family, and friendships come first this month and unstable relationships could come to an end.

November

In this 5 Year that focuses on adventure, progress, movement, and change, November is a 7 Personal Month. This is a time to clarify your goals and to work on the limiting beliefs that are holding you back from achieving them. The more you work on yourself in November, the better your results will be in December.

December

In this 5 Year that focuses on adventure, progress, movement, and change, December is an 8 Personal Month. This is a dynamic combination of numbers when anything can happen - and usually does. Be sure to maintain a positive mindset and put extra effort into manifesting your dreams.

Personal Year 6 - Personal Months

Love, Family, Domestic Responsibility

January

In this 6 Year that focuses on love, family, and domestic responsibility, January is a 7 Personal Month. This is a time to go within to work on self-awareness and personal development, and to examine the role you play in the relationships in your life. Observe what comes up and make positive changes.

February

In this 6 Year that focuses on love, family, and domestic responsibility, February is an 8 Personal Month. There may be progress in your career, and business opportunities could present themselves, especially if you work in a service-based career. Budget your finances and don't overspend.

March

In this 6 Year that focuses on love, family, and domestic responsibility, March is a 9 Personal Month. This is a time to forgive and bury the hatchet once and for all. Let go of what no longer serves you and release anyone from your life who prevents you from being happy.

April

In this 6 Year that focuses on love, family, and domestic responsibility, April is a 1 Personal Month. This can be a favorable time for singles to meet someone special. Be positive and proactive if you're looking for love. New opportunities will present themselves in all areas of your life.

May

In this 6 Year that focuses on love, family, and domestic responsibility, May is a 2 Personal Month. Relationship issues brewing beneath the surface will rise and need to be addressed this month with a partner, a family member, a work colleague, a neighbor, or a friend. Be diplomatic and compassionate.

June

In this 6 Year that focuses on love, family, and domestic responsibility, June is a 3 Personal Month. This is a time to lighten things up a bit, and to be a little more creative and have some fun. Be social, catch up with friends, and make time for creative hobbies and activities.

July

In this 6 Year that focuses on love, family, and domestic responsibility, July is a 4 Personal Month. This is a favorable time to make a commitment and to solidify things in your life. Be organized, disciplined, and work hard. It's a great time to renovate, redecorate, or do any type of work on the home.

August

In this 6 Year that focuses on love, family, and domestic responsibility, August is a 5 Personal Month. This is a time of movement, so if there's anything you want or need to change in your life, this is the month in which to do it. Expect the unexpected, especially regarding relationships and family matters.

September

In this 6 Year that focuses on love, family, and domestic responsibility, September is a 6 Personal Month. This is a period to devote your time and energy to friends, family, loved ones, and others in need. Be sympathetic and offer a helping hand where you can.

October

In this 6 Year that focuses on love, family, and domestic responsibility, October is a 7 Personal Month. This is a month for "you time," in which to rest and rejuvenate and contemplate the meaning (and direction) of your life. Focus on improving yourself inside and out and quieten your mind with some meditation.

November

In this 6 Year that focuses on love, family, and domestic responsibility, November is an 8 Personal Month. This can be a favorable time for business, especially for those in a service-based career. Budget your finances and don't overspend. Familiarize yourself with the Law of Attraction.

December

In this 6 Year that focuses on love, family, and domestic responsibility, December is a 9 Personal Month. Relationships that have been hanging on by a thread may finally unravel this month. This is a time of endings and transformation so that you can create a better you and a better life.

Personal Year 7 – Personal Months

Introspection, Personal and Spiritual Growth

January

In this 7 Year that focuses on introspection, and personal and spiritual growth, January is an 8 Personal Month. Despite your desire to go charging ahead, there is still a need for some fine-tuning behind the scenes. This is a month in which to get clear about what you want and to create a plan to achieve it. Focus on your finances and long-term career goals.

February

In this 7 Year that focuses on introspection, and personal and spiritual growth, February is a 9 Personal Month. This is a month of "ah-ha moments" and realizations that create a higher level of self-awareness. Be honest with yourself and let go of what no longer serves your greater good.

March

In this 7 Year that focuses on introspection, and personal and spiritual growth, March is a 1 Personal Month. This is a time to start something new, such as taking on a new project or investigating innovative and improved ways to live your life. Focus on your health and wellbeing and make lifestyle changes where needed.

April

In this 7 year that focuses on introspection, and personal and spiritual growth, April is a 2 Personal Month. This is a time to be patient if things don't happen as quickly as you would like. Be cooperative and diplomatic with others to avoid unnecessary conflict. Create balance in your life and express your emotions in a healthy way.

May

In this 7 year that focuses on introspection, and personal and spiritual growth, May is a 3 Personal Month. This is a time to identify what makes you unhappy so you can eliminate it from your life. Joy and personal happiness must be your major priority this month. Be social, have more fun and do things you enjoy.

June

In this 7 year that focuses on introspection, and personal and spiritual growth, June is a 4 Personal Month. This is a time to be productive and organized. Work hard and take care of the details in your personal life and career. Be proactive and disciplined, and you will reap the rewards.

July

In this 7 year that focuses on introspection, and personal and spiritual growth, July is a 5 Personal Month. Prepare for life to shake things up a bit, as this is a month of movement and change. Now's the right time to make any changes you need to put in motion. This is a beneficial time for travel and self-promotion.

August

In this 7 year that focuses on introspection, and personal and spiritual growth, August is a 6 Personal Month. Put time aside for domestic and family matters. Spend extra time with your partner, children, and other loved ones. This is a good month in which to renovate, redecorate, or work on your home.

September

In this 7 Year that focuses on introspection, and personal and spiritual growth, September is a 7 Personal Month. This is the ultimate time to get closer to God (Source, the Universe, the Divine). Allow yourself to reconnect with your spiritual side. Focus on self-improvement, spend time alone, and practice meditation.

October

In this 7 Year that focuses on introspection, and personal and spiritual growth, October is an 8 Personal Month. This is a time to recognize and reprogram any negative beliefs you may have about money. Adopt an attitude of abundance, be positive and proactive, and visualize your success.

November

In this 7 Year that focuses on introspection, and personal and spiritual growth, November is a 9 Personal Month. This is a good time to spring-clean your home - and your life. Get rid of unwanted items, people, behaviors, and beliefs and take steps toward improving your life. Let go and move on.

December

In this 7 Year that focuses on introspection, and personal and spiritual growth, December is a 1 Personal Month. New doors are opening and new opportunities will appear. Be courageous, ambitious, and proactive. Take the bull by the horns and don't miss out.

Personal Year 8 - Personal Months

Manifestation, Personal Power, Finances, Career

January

In this 8 Year that focuses on manifestation, personal power, finances, and careers, January is a 9 Personal Month. This is a month in which to let go of any old and outworn ideas that no longer serve you as you move forward into the new year - especially those relating to your finances and career.

February

In this 8 Year that focuses on manifestation, personal power, finances, and careers, February is a 1 Personal Month. This is a time to start new projects, be proactive, and take action. You can afford to be confident and ambitious. Don't hesitate to take opportunities when they arise.

March

In this 8 Year that focuses on manifestation, personal power, finances, and careers, March is a 2 Personal Month. You'll need to be cooperative if you want things to go your way, as negotiation may be required to receive the outcome you desire. It's a favorable time for singles to find love.

April

In this 8 Year that focuses on manifestation, personal power, finances, and careers, April is a 3 Personal Month. This is a social and busy time in which valuable contacts can be made (both business and personal). Follow up on good commercial ideas and creative solutions to problems.

May

In this 8 Year that focuses on manifestation, personal power, finances, and careers, May is a 4 Personal Month. This is a very busy time, so prepare for hard work. Pay attention to details, put in more hours, and go the extra mile - you'll be handsomely rewarded.

June

In this 8 Year that focuses on manifestation, personal power, finances, and careers, June is a 5 Personal Month. This is a dynamic time of change and rapid progress. Be flexible if things seem to come from "left field." It's a favorable time to advertise and promote yourself.

July

In this 8 Year that focuses on manifestation, personal power, finances, and careers, July is a 6 Personal Month. This can be a rewarding time for business advancement, especially for those working in service-based careers. Put time aside to focus on relationship and family matters.

August

In this 8 Year that focuses on manifestation, personal power, finances, and careers, August is a 7 Personal Month. This isn't a time to force big moves. Instead, take a step back, refocus, and regroup. Spend some quiet time alone for contemplation, rest, and relaxation.

September

In this 8 Year that focuses on manifestation, personal power, finances, and careers, September is an 8 Personal Month. This is a powerful manifestation cycle, so focus on what you want and be positive at all times. Be courageous and ambitious, and put extra effort into manifesting your dreams.

October

In this 8 Year that focuses on manifestation, personal power, finances, and careers, October is a 9 Personal Month. This is a time to re-evaluate what's working for you and what isn't, so you can make adjustments. Don't be afraid to leave the past behind as a better life lies ahead.

November

In this 8 Year that focuses on manifestation, personal power, finances, and careers, November is a 1 Personal Month. It's full steam ahead as new opportunities present themselves. Be decisive, don't hesitate or sit on the fence. Take a fresh approach to everything you do.

December

In this 8 Year that focuses on manifestation, personal power, finances, and careers, December is a 2 Personal Month. Use your heightened sensitivity and intuition to your advantage by following your instincts at all times. Be patient. Don't force things to happen. Singles could meet someone special.

Personal Year 9 – Personal Months

Transformation, Completion, Endings

January

In this 9 Year that focuses on transformation, completion, and endings, January is a 1 Personal Month. This is a time to make changes and improvements in all areas of your life. Get a makeover, start a new job, begin a new, healthier regime – anything that enhances your wellbeing and quality of life.

February

In this 9 Year that focuses on transformation, completion, and endings, February is a 2 Personal Month. This can be an emotional time for some, so be gentle on yourself and others. Relationship issues will surface to be reviewed and troubled relationships may come to an end.

March

In this 9 Year that focuses on transformation, completion, and endings, March is a 3 Personal Month. This is a time to be social and catch up with friends. It is also a period in which to get things off your chest and to communicate how you're truly feeling inside. Be diplomatic and speak your truth.

April

In this 9 Year that focuses on transformation, completion, and endings, April is a 4 Personal Month. This is a time to plan your life the way you want it to be and to take action toward making it a reality. Get everything in order in your personal life and career. Face and overcome any challenges.

May

In this 9 Year that focuses on transformation, completion, and endings, May is a 5 Personal Month. This is a time of significant change and movement. Some changes will be expected and others will not – either way, trust in the divine order of events and go with the flow.

June

In this 9 Year that focuses on transformation, completion, and endings, June is a 6 Personal Month. This is a time to focus on your family and relationships. Existing relationship problems will come to a head and will require your attention. This is a favorable time for business.

July

In this 9 year that focuses on transformation, completion,

and endings, July is a 7 Personal Month. This is a time to go within to work on your personal development. Meditation, yoga and other practices that enable you to reach a higher level of awareness are favorable.

August

In this 9 year that focuses on transformation, completion, and endings, August is an 8 Personal Month. This is a month in which to reclaim your personal power over anyone or anything that causes you to feel disempowered. This a great time to make business or career changes.

September

In this 9 Year that focuses on transformation, completion, and endings, September is a 9 Personal Month. This month you'll get a double dose of endings and transformation so be extra diligent about letting go of what no longer serves you. Get rid of outdated and negative beliefs that hold you back.

October

In this 9 Year that focuses on transformation, completion, and endings, October is a 1 Personal Month. New doors will open for you this month so have the courage to walk through them. You'll feel revitalized and renewed. Take advantage of this fresh energy and your optimistic attitude.

November

In this 9 Year that focuses on transformation, completion, and endings, November is a 2 Personal Month. This is a time to address your emotional side. New experiences may create new emotions, or repressed emotions from the past may surface to be resolved and released.

December

In this 9 Year that focuses on transformation, completion, and endings, December is a 3 Personal Month. This is a month of social activity and celebration. Take a vacation if you can and make time to catch up with friends. Go out of your way to have fun and lift your spirits. Be playful.

Now, let's move on to the Personal Day Number.

The Personal Day Number

The Personal Day Number gives an indication of the energy of your day. Even though its influence is subtle and mild in comparison to the Personal Year and Personal Month Numbers, it pays to bear it in mind when making important plans and decisions.

How to calculate the Personal Day Number

Step 1: Add your Personal Month Number to the calendar day you're enquiring about.

Step 2: Add any double-digit numbers together to get a single-digit Personal Day Number between 1 and 9.

For example, to find the Personal Day Number for the 9th if you're in a 1 Personal Month, the calculation would be:

1 (Personal Month Number) + 9 (Calendar Day Number) = 10

1+0 = **1 Personal Day Number**

Therefore the 9th is a 1 Personal Day in a 1 Personal Month.

To follow table shows Calendar Day Numbers to get you started.

Calendar Day Numbers			
1st = 1	9th = 9	17th = 8	25th = 7
2nd = 2	10th = 1	18th = 9	26th = 8
3rd = 3	11th = 2	19th = 1	27th = 9
4th = 4	12th = 3	20th = 2	28th = 1
5th = 5	13th = 4	21st = 3	29th = 2
6th = 6	14th = 5	22nd = 4	30th = 3
7th = 7	15th = 6	23rd = 5	31st = 4
8th = 8	16th = 7	24th = 6	

Personal Day Number tips

Here are some tips on how to make the most of your Personal Day:

Personal Day Number 1

- Be assertive and courageous
- Take charge
- Start something new
- Be proactive
- Embrace your independence
- Make yourself number one

Personal Day Number 2

- Cooperate with others
- Be patient and slow down
- Follow your intuition

- Express your emotions in a healthy way
- Embrace your sensitivity
- Connect with loved ones

Personal Day Number 3

- Be playful and have fun
- Connect with friends
- Do something creative
- Express yourself
- Communicate your feelings
- Speak your truth

Personal Day Number 4

- Work hard
- Get everything in order
- Complete unfinished business
- Be organized and disciplined
- Take action
- Be productive

Personal Day Number 5

- Be flexible
- Make changes
- Network and promote yourself
- Be adventurous

- Have fun and be social
- Try new things

Personal Day Number 6

- Fulfill your obligations
- Be responsible
- Make time for those in need
- Spend time with loved ones and family
- Be of service to others
- Focus on health and beauty

Personal Day Number 7

- Spend quiet time alone
- Study
- Meditate, do yoga or qi gong
- Get out in nature
- Focus on your health and wellbeing
- Embrace your spiritual side

Personal Day Number 8

- Budget your finances
- Be ambitious
- Work hard
- Pay your bills

- Put effort in at work
- Be positive

Personal Day Number 9

- Be of service to others
- Do something for charity
- Let go of things you don't want
- Be tolerant and patient
- Forgive others and the past
- Do something creative

Interesting fact

Be mindful of when you're in the same Personal Day Number as your Personal Year or Personal Month, as you'll experience a double dose of that energy and all that it represents.

The Universal Year Number

The Universal Year Number (also known as the World Year Number) is the total of the current calendar year: for example: 2016 (2+0+1+6) = 9 Universal Year Number. You can think of the Universal Year Number as the Personal Year Number for the world, which influences humanity as a whole.

Because a forecasting number has the same meaning wherever it appears, the Universal Year Numbers have the same meanings as the Personal Year Numbers, except they apply to the world rather than an individual. When you take the Universal Year Number into consideration alongside the other cycle numbers in your chart, you gain a broader understanding of the energies influencing your life.

Here is a brief outline of the Universal Year Number meanings:

1 Universal Year Number – New Beginnings and Action

2 Universal Year Number – Cooperation and Balance

3 Universal Year Number – Communication and Expression

4 Universal Year Number – Building and Planning

5 Universal Year Number – Movement and Change

6 Universal Year Number – Responsibility and Universal Love

7 Universal Year Number – Introspection and Personal Growth

8 Universal Year Number – Karmic Justice and Power

9 Universal Year Number – Endings and Completions

Interesting fact

Not only is there a Universal Year Number, but there are a Universal Month and a Universal Day Number, too.

Here are the calculation formulas for those:

Universal Month Number = Universal Year Number + Calendar Month Number

Universal Day Number = Universal Month Number + Calendar Day Number

The Universal Month and Universal Day Numbers have the same meanings as the Personal Month and Personal Day Numbers, except they apply to the world rather than an individual.

Even though your Personal Month and Personal Day Numbers affect you the most, it pays to know the Universal Month and Universal Day Numbers when planning major events – just for good measure.

Now let's move on to the other long-term cycles that are currently influencing your life – the Pinnacles and Challenges.

Pinnacles and Challenge Numbers and Their Meanings

As you go through your life there are four distinct periods of development called Pinnacles. A Pinnacle (also known as a Peak Number) is a period of growth and advancement that provides you with an opportunity to expand in a particular area. When you utilize the opportunities a Pinnacle presents, you're one step closer to fulfilling your destiny and life purpose.

Each of the four Pinnacles has an accompanying Challenge. In other words, there are four specific obstacles that must be overcome for you to reach your full potential. Your Challenges are the lessons you must learn on your journey towards self-mastery. Think of it this way: A Pinnacle is a "gateway" that leads you toward your greatest potential for success, but you can only make it through once you've overcome its accompanying Challenge.

How to calculate the Pinnacle Numbers

You have four Pinnacles in your numerology chart that are calculated from your birth date. First, begin by reducing the month, day, and year numbers of your birth date down to three single-digit numbers (unless they total 11 or 22).

If you have an 11 or 22 month, day, or year – that is, if you were born in November (11); on the 11th, 22nd, or 29th of your birth month, or in a year that totals 11 or 22, such as 1975 (1 + 9 + 7 + 5 = 22) – it doesn't reduce down to 2 or 4 but rather remains 11 or 22.

- This is the formula to calculate your four Pinnacle Numbers:
- **First Pinnacle:** Month of birth + day of birth; reduce to a single number unless it's 11 or 22
- **Second Pinnacle:** Day of birth + year of birth; reduce to a single number unless it's 11 or 22
- **Third Pinnacle:** First pinnacle + second pinnacle; reduce to a single number unless it's 11 or 22
- **Fourth Pinnacle:** Month of birth + year of birth; reduce to a single number unless it's 11 or 22

How to calculate the Challenge Numbers

You have four Challenges in your numerology chart also calculated from your birth date. The only difference between calculating the Pinnacles and Challenges is that we use *addition* for the Pinnacles and *subtraction* for the Challenges. Because we're subtracting numbers, it's perfectly normal to end up with a 0 or negative (–) Challenge Number.

First, we begin by reducing the month, day, and year numbers of your birth date down to three single-digit numbers. If you have an 11 or a 22 in your birth date, this is one instance in numerology where they must be reduced down to single-digit numbers 2 and 4. For example, if you were born in November or on the 11th day of the month, both the month and the day numbers would reduce down to 2.

When you're subtracting a larger number from a smaller number, simply find the difference between the numbers and that is your Challenge Number - for example, 3 - (minus) 8 = 5 because 5 is the difference between 3 and 8.

This is the formula to calculate your four Challenge Numbers:

First Challenge: Month of birth - (minus) day of birth; or find the difference by subtracting the smaller number from the larger number

Second Challenge: Day of birth - (minus) year of birth; or find the difference by subtracting the smaller number from the larger number

Third Challenge: First Challenge - (minus) second Challenge; or find the difference by subtracting the smaller number from the larger number

Fourth Challenge: Month of birth - (minus) year of birth; or find the difference by subtracting the smaller number from the larger number

Pinnacle and Challenge Number Periods

Now let's take a look at the Pinnacle and Challenge Number Periods.

The Pinnacle and Challenge Number Periods are determined by your Life Path Number and the formula for calculating them is very easy. To calculate your First Pinnacle Period simply subtract your Life Path Number from 36 (11/2, 22/4, and 33/6 Life Path Numbers reduce down to 2, 4, and 6). For example, the First Pinnacle Period for a 3 Life Path would be 0 to 33 years because 3 subtracted from 36 is 33.

To calculate your Second, Third, and Fourth Pinnacle Periods, simply add 9 years to the ending age of the preceding Pinnacle. To make it easier for you, I've listed your Pinnacle and Challenge Periods in the table below.

Life Path Number	1st Pinnacle/ Challenge Ages	2nd Pinnacle/ Challenge Ages	3rd Pinnacle/ Challenge Ages	4th Pinnacle/ Challenge Ages
1	0 to 35yr	36 to 44yr	45 to 53yr	54yr +
2	0 to 34yr	35 to 43yr	44 to 52yr	53yr +
3	0 to 33yr	34 to 42yr	43 to 51yr	52yr +
4	0 to 32yr	33 to 41yr	42 to 50yr	51yr +
5	0 to 31yr	32 to 40yr	41 to 49yr	50yr +
6	0 to 30yr	31 to 39yr	40 to 48yr	49yr +
7	0 to 29yr	30 to 38yr	39 to 47yr	48yr +
8	0 to 28yr	29 to 37yr	38 to 46yr	47yr +
9	0 to 27yr	28 to 36yr	37 to 45yr	46yr +
11/2	0 to 34yr	35 to 43yr	44 to 52yr	53yr +
22/4	0 to 32yr	33 to 41yr	42 to 50yr	51yr +
33/6	0 to 30yr	31 to 39yr	40 to 48yr	49yr +

Interesting fact

The 2nd and 3rd Pinnacle and Challenge Number Periods are of the shortest duration, being only 9 years each, whereas the 1st and 4th Periods extend over longer periods of time.

Now let's take a look at the Pinnacle and Challenge Number Meanings, starting with the Pinnacles.

Pinnacle Number 1

Strength, Independence, Leadership

During this pinnacle, life provides you with the opportunity to become independent and self-reliant. You will gain the courage to walk your own path and the confidence to be your true, authentic self. You'll find yourself less concerned with others' opinions of you and more concerned with pleasing yourself. There is potential for you to become a leader during this time or to start your own business or project. This is an opportunity to break away from the pack, so you can march to the beat of your own drum. Providing you are assertive, confident, and considerate toward others, there is potential for happiness and success.

Pinnacle Number 2

Relationships, Co-operation, Intuition

During this pinnacle, life provides you with the opportunity to develop harmonious relationships and a deeper understanding of others. You will gain the ability to know instinctively what people need along with the steps that must be taken to help them. Your intuition will be strong and you'll be more sensitive to energy, your environment, and the people around you. This is a favorable time to study metaphysics, health, healing, counseling, art, music, or anything that involves helping people. Providing you are balanced, assertive, diplomatic, and cooperative when dealing with others, there is potential for happiness and success.

Pinnacle Number 3

Self-expression, Communication, Creativity

During this pinnacle, life provides you with the opportunity to develop your artistic and creative abilities. You will gain the ability to communicate and express yourself more easily and effectively, and may choose to do this through speaking, writing, performing, singing, creating, or designing. It doesn't matter *how* you do it, as any form of self-expression is favorable during this time. Providing you are confident, disciplined, focused, don't scatter your energies, and dedicate yourself to the job at hand, there is potential for happiness and success.

Pinnacle Number 4

Discipline, Order, Foundation

During this pinnacle, life provides you with the opportunity to create stability and build a solid foundation for your future. You will gain the ability to persevere through your challenges and overcome the obstacles that you face. This time will help you to be organized, disciplined, and focused so you can achieve your goals and make something of your life. Providing you work hard, have a good work ethic and a positive mindset, dedicate yourself to the job at hand, and finish what you start, there is potential for happiness and success.

Pinnacle Number 5

Communication, Change, Experience

During this pinnacle, life provides you with the opportunity to expand your life experience and explore the world around you. You will gain the ability to communicate more effectively with others and many new people will cross your path. Life will send you many new and exciting experiences and you will learn the importance of self-discipline and moderation. There will be opportunities to promote yourself and to adapt to the many changes you undergo. Providing you are flexible, adaptable, grounded, disciplined, and focused, there is potential for happiness and success.

Pinnacle Number 6

Service, Family, Domestic Responsibility

During this pinnacle, life provides you with the opportunity to take more responsibility and be of service to your loved ones, family, friends, and community. You will gain the ability to balance giving with receiving and your home life with your career as you learn to balance other's needs with your own. This is a favorable time to make a commitment, get married, have children, take care of family, or to work in a service- or home-based business. Providing you are responsible, compassionate, kind, and caring toward others, there is potential for happiness and success.

Pinnacle Number 7

Personal Development, Spirituality, Specialization

During this pinnacle, life provides you with the opportunity to investigate, study, and become a specialist in your craft. You will gain the ability to develop a deeper understanding of yourself, your talents, and the deeper meaning of life. During this time you will be encouraged to reach a higher level of awareness through personal development and spiritual teachings. This is a favorable time to study and explore metaphysics and/or alternative modalities. Providing you develop and trust your intuition and adopt a spiritual practice, there is potential for happiness and success.

Pinnacle Number 8

Personal Power, Finances, Career

During this pinnacle, life provides you with the opportunity for financial and material gain, providing you are honest in your dealings, work hard, and make good decisions. You will gain the ability to rise to a position of authority, reclaim your personal power, or possibly start your own business. During this time life will encourage you to master your ego, adopt a positive mindset, and develop a healthy relationship with money. Providing you are honest, work hard, are organized, enterprising, ambitious, and strong - there is potential for happiness and success.

Pinnacle Number 9

Broadmindedness, Service, Compassion

During this pinnacle, life provides you with the opportunity to develop broad-mindedness, compassion, and tolerance through selfless service to others. You will gain the ability to develop a deeper understanding of people combined with a desire to want to help them improve their lives. During this time, life will encourage you to accept, forgive, and release your pain of the past and accept that endings are a natural part of life. Providing you learn to put others' needs above your own and can understand the interconnectedness of all things, there is potential for happiness and success.

Pinnacle Number 11/2 *(also read Pinnacle Number 2, see page 187)*

Illumination, Transformation, Spiritual Awakening

During this pinnacle, life provides you with the opportunity to reach a higher level of awareness and to inspire others with ease. You will gain the ability to enhance and follow your intuition as you work toward improving yourself and living by your higher ideals. During this time you will gain self-confidence and wisdom. This is a favorable time for spiritual expansion, personal transformation, and developing your psychic abilities. Depending on the other numbers in your chart there is also potential for recognition and fame. Providing you can balance your emotions, master your sensitivity, and are driven to serve the greater good, there is potential for happiness and success.

Pinnacle Number 22/4 *(also read Pinnacle Number 4, page 188)*

Commitment, Achievement, Humanitarianism

During this pinnacle life provides you with the opportunity to implement, manage, or support an endeavor that serves the community or humanity as a whole. You will gain the ability to apply your vision combined with your organizational and managerial skills toward something of great importance. During this time you'll be encouraged to "think big" and may be drawn toward promoting national or international affairs. This is a highly productive time and providing you have a clear vision, dedicate yourself entirely to your goals, and have the endurance and stamina to follow through, there is potential for happiness and success.

Pinnacle Number 33/6 *(also read Pinnacle Number 6, page 189)*

Commitment, Achievement, Establishment

During this pinnacle, life provides you with the opportunity to utilize your healing abilities in service to others. You will gain the ability to heal others and yourself through love, understanding, and the use of spiritual principles. During this time there will be much responsibility and self-sacrifice as you learn to use love as an energetic force for change. This is a favorable time for teaching or studying the healing arts, reaching self-mastery and personal transformation, and developing a broader understanding of people and life. Providing you can master your emotions and depersonalize the pain you see in the world, there is potential for happiness and success.

Interesting fact

Most numerologists don't recognize the 33/6 Pinnacle Number; however I've included it anyway. A 33/6 Pinnacle can only occur when we add a 22/4 and an 11/2 together and most numerologists reduce this down to a 6 Pinnacle Number.

Next, we're moving on to the Challenge Number meanings.

Challenge Number 0

Choice, Opportunity, Free Will

A 0 Challenge Number indicates no specific challenges; however you're not completely off the hook, as life will still put obstacles in your path. The 0 Challenge Number indicates a challenge of choice, so it is your decision whether you want to live to your highest potential or simply cruise along. It's up to you which way you choose.

Challenge Number 1

Assertiveness, Independence, Confidence

During this period, life will challenge you to become more assertive and to stand up for yourself. You will learn to be independent and less concerned with others' opinions of you. The more you trust and believe in yourself, the more confident you will be. You may find it challenging to walk your own path, but you were born with the ability to do so.

Challenge Number 2

Sensitivity, Balance, Emotions

During this period, life will challenge you to master your sensitivity and balance your emotions. You will learn not to overreact or to take things too personally as you work towards developing your self-confidence. The more you believe in yourself the less jealous you will be of others. You may find it a challenge to overcome your inferiority complex but you were born with the ability to do so.

Challenge Number 3

Self-expression, Communication, Focus

During this period, life will challenge you to express yourself positively and effectively. Rather than use communication to exaggerate, gossip, criticize, and complain, you'll be encouraged to use your words to bring understanding, happiness, inspiration, and hope. You will also learn to focus and not scatter yourself in too many directions at once, so you can achieve your goals. You may find it a challenge to identify your feelings and put them into words, but you were born with the ability to do so.

Challenge Number 4

Discipline, Perseverance, Building

During this period, life will challenge you to be disciplined, organized, and focused in every area of your life. Rather than procrastinate, give up, or walk away from your problems, you'll be encouraged to persevere through obstacles so you can face your challenges head on. You will also learn to be patient as you gradually build a solid and stable foundation. You may find it a challenge to be positive in the face of adversity, but you were born with the ability to do so.

Challenge Number 5

Freedom, Commitment, Moderation

During this period, life will challenge you to master your desire to overindulge in physical pleasures of the senses. When it comes to sex, spending money, or consuming alcohol and/or food, medication and/or drugs, you will learn that abstinence or moderation is the key. Rather than becoming a rolling stone or a jack of all trades and specialist of none, you are being encouraged to stick at one thing and follow it through. You may find it a challenge to commit fully to others, your responsibilities, and your goals, but you were born with the ability to do so.

Challenge Number 6

Acceptance, Idealism, Responsibility

During this period, life will challenge you to become less opinionated and self-righteous and more accepting of others and yourself. Rather than be overly idealistic about what is right and wrong, you will learn to acknowledge that others are free to live as they choose. During this time you will also be encouraged to accept the imperfection in yourself, others, and the world. You may find it a challenge to take responsibility for your actions, but you were born with the ability to do so.

Challenge Number 7

Spirituality, Trust, Self-awareness

During this period, you will be challenged to look beyond superficiality to explore the deeper meaning of life. You will also be encouraged to trust and have faith in yourself, others, and a higher purpose. During this time you will learn that self-awareness and transformation are the key to living a more fulfilled life and that true happiness can only come from within. You may find it a challenge to spend time alone without feeling lonely, but you were born with the ability to do so.

Challenge Number 8

Ego, Personal Power, Materialism

During this period, life will challenge you to overcome your desire for power, success, recognition, the accumulation of material possessions, and wealth. As you learn to master your ego, you will also be encouraged to balance the material and spiritual aspects of your life. During this time you will learn to reclaim your personal power and be less controlling of others You may find it a challenge to form a healthy relationship with money, but you were born with the ability to do so.

Interesting fact

It's impossible to have a 9 Challenge Number – because 9 is the highest single digit, it cannot be subtracted from to still leave 9 as a remainder.

Be mindful of your challenges but don't dwell on them. They are simply there to help you to evolve and grow. As challenging as your life may be at times, remember that your soul has chosen this in advance and you have the strength and ability to overcome everything that is placed in front of you. By facing your challenges head on with courage and determination, you will improve your quality of life. No soul is given more than they can handle - and that applies to you!

Major Life Cycle Numbers and Their Meanings

Also known as Life Cycles, Growth Cycles or Period Cycles, Major Life Cycles divide your Life Path Number journey into three blocks of time that highlight the three stages of growth throughout your life. These three stages of growth are often called the Cycles of Youth, Maturity, and Wisdom. Each Major Life Cycle Number has its own unique theme designed for your personal growth, but because a forecasting number has the same meaning wherever it appears, the descriptions are the same as the Personal Year and Pinnacles, for example.

You can think of your three Major Life Cycles as the three areas of development that will help you fulfill your destiny as your journey along your life path. Throughout a Major Life Cycle period, its accompanying Pinnacle and Challenge Numbers represent the opportunities and challenges that will be encountered along that path.

How to Calculate the Major Life Cycle Numbers

The three Major Life Cycle Numbers are calculated from your birth date. First, begin by reducing the month, day, and year numbers of your birth date down to three single-digit numbers, unless they total 11 or 22.

If you have an 11 or 22 month, day, or year – that is, if you were born in November (11); on the 11th, 22nd, or 29th of your birth month; or in a year that totals 11 or 22, such as 1975 (1 + 9 + 7 + 5 = 22) – it doesn't reduce down to 2 or 4 but rather remains 11 or 22.

Let's use the birth date December 11, 1969 (12–11–1969), as an example:

1+2 / 11 / 1+9+6+9 = 25

3 11 2+5

7

Therefore, the three single digits for birth date 12–11–1969 are 3, 11, and 7.

Interesting fact

Your three Major Life Cycle Numbers are the same 3 single-digit numbers from your Life Path Number calculation, using the reducing-down method (*see page* 7). This is another reason why master numerologists believe the reducing-down method is the most accurate Life Path Number calculation method to use.

The three Major Life Cycle Numbers are as follows:

- First Major Life Cycle Number: Your **month** of birth = Cycle of Youth Number
- Second Major Life Cycle Number: Your **day** of birth = Cycle of Maturity Number

- Third Major Life Cycle Number: Your **year** of birth = Cycle of Wisdom Number

In our example for birth date 12 -11-1969, the First Major Life Cycle Number is **3**, the Second Major Life Cycle Number is **11**, and the Third Major Life Cycle Number is **7**.

Major Life Cycle Number periods

Now, let's take a look at the Major Life Cycle Number Periods.

There are several theories about the Major Life Cycle Periods; however the chart below, based upon the Life Path Number, is the most accurate and commonly used of all.

Locate your Life Path Number to find the ages of your Major Life Cycle Periods.

Life Path Number	First Cycle Ages	Second Cycle Ages	Third Cycle Ages
1	0-26yr	27-53yr	54yr+
2 and 11	0-25yr	26-52yr	53yr+
3	0-33yr	34-60yr	61yr+
4 and 22	0-32yr	33-59yr	60yr+
5	0-31yr	32-58yr	59yr+
6 and 33	0-30yr	31-57yr	58yr+
7	0-29yr	30-56yr	57yr+
8	0-28yr	29-55yr	56yr+
9	0-27yr	28-54yr	55yr+

We'll now move on to the Major Life Cycle Number meanings which apply to your first, second, and third cycle numbers.

Major Life Cycle Number 1

Independence, Leadership, Courage

A 1 Major Life Cycle will encourage you to be more independent and stand on your own two feet. It will show you how to demonstrate your leadership abilities, trust your decisions, and walk your own path. Over this period of time you'll gain inner strength, courage, and self-confidence. You'll become less concerned with others' opinions and learn not to compromise who you truly are to keep others happy. This is a favorable cycle in which to: start a business, be self-employed, begin a new project, have a makeover, take on a leadership role, advance your career, and create/invent something unique.

Major Life Cycle Number 2

Cooperation, Balance, Emotions

A 2 Major Life Cycle will encourage you to be more co-operative, compassionate, and sensitive toward others. It will teach you how to mediate and compromise, so you can harmonize more effectively with the people around you. Over this period of time you'll explore and expand your emotional side and learn to balance your life. You'll also be given the opportunity to enhance your intuition and psychic abilities. This is a favorable cycle in which to: go into partnership, commit to a relationship, be of service to others, get married, start a family, and develop a musical or creative talent.

Major Life Cycle Number 3

Self-expression, Communication, Creativity

A 3 Major Life Cycle will encourage you to use your creativity and imagination in all areas of your life. It will teach you how to express yourself verbally, artistically, intellectually, physically, and emotionally in a positive way as opposed to expressing yourself negatively. Over this period of time you'll learn to communicate more effectively and develop any creative talent you may have and possibly turn it into a career. This is a favorable cycle in which to: start a hobby, learn an instrument, write a book (blog or poetry), journal, sing (or express yourself in other ways), develop your artistic/creative talents, and be social.

Major Life Cycle Number 4

Discipline, Effort, Building

A 4 Major Life Cycle will encourage you to work hard to build a solid foundation for your future. It will teach you the value of dedication, discipline, and organization so you can make something of your life. Over this period of time you'll learn how to overcome obstacles and persevere through the challenges that cross your path. You'll discover that effort brings rewards as you work toward achieving your goals. This is a favorable cycle in which to: start a business or build a career, build or renovate a home, make a commitment, get married, and save money.

Major Life Cycle Number 5

Life Experience, Progress, Adaptability

A 5 Major Life Cycle will encourage you to be more adaptable and go with the flow of life. It will teach you the value of personal freedom and the importance of moderation and discipline. Many people, experiences, and unexpected events will cross your path as you develop a broader understanding of others and of life. Over this period of time you'll learn to promote yourself and communicate more effectively. This is a favorable cycle in which to: travel, move house, try new things, promote yourself, and make big changes.

Major Life Cycle Number 6

Relationships, Family, Domestic Responsibility

A 6 Major Life Cycle will encourage you to accept responsibility, especially relating to your loved ones, family, and career. It will teach you how to be of service and to put others' needs above your own. During this time you'll learn many lessons in relationships and love. You'll also discover how to define your personal boundaries and find a healthy balance between giving and receiving. This is a favorable cycle in which to: get married, have children, dedicate to family, and work in a service-based career.

Major Life Cycle Number 7

Specialization, Personal Development, Spiritual Growth

A 7 Major Life Cycle will encourage you to look beyond the superficial toward the deeper and more meaningful things in life. It will enable you to reach a higher level of consciousness through personal development and spiritual understanding. During this time you'll learn to focus and specialize in your craft. You'll discover how to be alone without feeling lonely and to value your relationship with the Divine. This is a favorable cycle in which to: study, adopt a spiritual practice, explore alternative modalities, work on self-improvement, and develop your intuition and psychic abilities.

Major Life Cycle Number 8

Personal Power, Finances, Career

An 8 Major Life Cycle will encourage you to recognize and reprogram your negative beliefs about money and life. It will also enable you to take on a leadership role and make headway in your career. During this time you'll learn to stand up for yourself and take charge. Providing you work hard and have a healthy relationship with money you can attract abundance and success. This is a favorable cycle in which to: make money, start a business, explore self-employment, take on a leadership role, advance your career, make a sound investment, and deal with legal matters.

Major Life Cycle Number 9

Service, Transformation, Forgiveness

A 9 Major Life Cycle will encourage you to be more tolerant, compassionate, and understanding toward others. It will enable you to develop broad-mindedness as you come into contact with people from all walks of life. During this time you'll be encouraged to heal and forgive your misfortunes of the past. You'll learn to be of service to others and to develop a global world-view. This is a favorable cycle in which to: support a cause, serve the community, develop an artistic or a creative talent, heal past wounds, and improve family relations.

Major Life Cycle Number 11/2

Illumination, Transformation, Spiritual Awareness

An 11/2 Major Life Cycle will encourage you to raise your consciousness through personal development and transformation. As you transform yourself, you'll be encouraged to help others do the same. During this time you will learn to find harmony within yourself as you uplift and inspire those around you. This is a favorable cycle in which to: develop your spiritual awareness, enhance your intuition and psychic abilities, study any form of psychology, counselling, or healing, explore mind/body/spirit, work in a service-based career, and specialize in your craft.

(*See also Major Life Cycle Number 2, page 202*)

Major Life Cycle Number 22/4

Commitment, Achievement, Establishment

A 22/4 Major Life Cycle will encourage you to do something of benefit for the workplace, community, or humanity as a whole. You may create or be involved with a project, organization, product, or service that bridges the conventional and alternative worlds. During this time you'll learn to apply yourself, work hard, and focus, as you put your talents to good use. This is a favorable cycle in which to: think globally, take on a leadership role, support a cause, serve the community or humanity as a whole, be inventive, and look at ways of improving society.

(*See also Major Life Cycle Number 4, page 203*)

SUMMARY OF FORECASTING NUMBERS

Now that you've calculated all of your cycles, let's take a look at all of your Forecasting Numbers together:

Personal Year Number this year ________

Personal Year Number next year ________

Universal Year Number this year ________

Universal Year Number next year ________

Personal Month Numbers:

Jan _______ Feb_________ Mar _________ Apr ________

May _______ June ________ Jul _______ Aug _________

Sep _________ Oct ________ Nov _______ Dec ________

Pinnacle Numbers:

1st _______ 2nd_________ 3rd _________ 4th ________

Challenge Numbers:

1st _______ 2nd_________ 3rd _________ 4th ________

Pinnacle/Challenge Number Periods:

1st ______ to _______ 2nd _____ to ______

3rd ______ to ______ 4th _____ to _____

Major Life Cycle Numbers:

1st _______ 2nd _________ 3rd _________

Major Life Cycle Number Periods:

1st ______ to _______ 2nd _____ to ______

3rd ______ to ______

Part IV

OTHER NUMBERS AROUND YOU

In addition to Personality Numbers and Forecasting Numbers that influence your life, there are numbers around you that contribute to your experiences and environment, too. We'll explore some of them in this part of the book.

Business Name, Website, and Other Name Numbers

It isn't only a person's name that has an energy vibration – a business name, a website domain name, a rock band's name, a pet's name, a book title, a television program's name, a product name, all have an energy vibration, too. In fact, everything that has a name also has a number and that number sends an energetic message to the world.

When choosing a name, whether it's for a business, website, pet, book, band, product or anything else, be sure to calculate its number, so you know the type of vibration it's giving off. Specific numbers are perfect for certain projects – for example, 3 is a creative number, therefore it's the perfect number for any type of creative project or business. 6 and 9 are numbers of "service," therefore they're ideal for a service-based business or website.

A name number is calculated by using the exact same formula used to calculate the Destiny Number (*see page 10*).

Name Number descriptions

1 Name

A 1 name promotes individuality, leadership, and innovation. It's the ideal number for something you wish to be original and unique, or a front-runner/market leader in its field. This number is best suited to something that isn't reliant on, or involved in, any kind of partnership, as it is very much an individual energy. This is a pioneering, action-orientated, and creative number.

2 Name

A 2 name promotes harmony, healing, and meaningful connections with others. It's the ideal number for something that helps or heals people, animals, the land, an area or space, or the environment. This is a good number for anything musical or creative, or anything that requires balance, meditation, or negotiation. This is also a number of counseling, service, and cooperation.

3 Name

A 3 name promotes communication, self-expression, and creativity. It's the ideal number for anything relating to communication, promotion, and sales. This is a good number for any type of creative endeavor or anything that involves (or relates to) the literary, creative, visual, or performing arts. This is also a number of humor, joy, fun, and entertainment, which is also suitable for anything relating to children, music, and color.

4 Name

A 4 name promotes organization, stability, and order. It's the ideal number for anything that involves building, planning, managing, analyzing, and strategizing. This is a good number for anything relating to structure or the land, such as construction, landscaping, building, engineering, or architecture. Anything that creates order, such as coaching, accounting, banking, town planning, business training, or auditing, can thrive under this number.

5 Name

A 5 name promotes innovation, progressive change, and breaking new ground. It's the ideal number for anything that relates to event planning, project management, travel, media, communication, advertising, networking, and PR. This is a good number for hospitality, entertainment, and public speaking, as well as anything that relates to marketing, consulting, advising, informing, networking, and spreading the word.

6 Name

A 6 name promotes harmony, healing, and love. It's the ideal number for anything creative or that relates to food, nutrition, fashion, beauty, or health. Childcare, teaching, coaching, and counseling endeavors can thrive under this number. This is the ideal number for decorators, designers, musicians, writers, actors, and artists. This is also a good number for a home-based business or anything service-related.

7 Name

A 7 name promotes health, wellbeing, personal development, and higher learning. It's the ideal number for anything scientific, technical, educational, spiritual, or metaphysical. Anything psychology-based, such as counseling and coaching, can thrive under this number. 7 provokes a search for truth, so it's a good number for anything that involves researching, studying, reporting, strategizing, and analyzing.

8 Name

An 8 name promotes personal power, leadership, and management. It is the ideal number for anything that relates to property, banking, investing, finance, and corporate business. The number 8 balances the scales of justice, so it's a good number for law and mediation. 8 is also a karmic number so any endeavor with this number must operate with honesty and integrity in order to thrive. This is a good number for self-employment.

9 Name

A 9 name promotes humanitarianism, charity, and universal love. It is the ideal number for anything service-related that assists the community or humanity as a whole, such as education, health and wellbeing, healing, social services, and law. 9 is a creative number, so it is suitable for decorators, designers, musicians, writers, actors, and artists. This is a good number for supporting a national or international movement or cause.

House and Apartment Numbers

Just like people, businesses, and names, a house has an energy vibration too. This vibration is determined by its House Number. Even though the numerology profiles of the people inhabiting the home have the strongest influence of all, the House Number will still have an effect on its inhabitants. When you understand the nature of your House Number, you can accentuate the positives and minimize the challenges within the home.

How to calculate a House Number

To calculate a House Number, simply add the numbers in the street address together and then reduce them to a single-digit House Number between 1 and 9.

For example, 4506 Main Street would be:

4+5+0+6 = 15

1+5 = 6 House Number

Apartment Numbers

When calculating a House Number for an apartment, the number of the apartment is the House Number. For example, Apartment 6 at 564 Main Street is a 6 House Number because 6 is the apartment number.

When the apartment number includes a letter, for example Apartment 32B at 564 Main Street, the letter must be converted to a number and calculated with the remaining apartment number/s. So the above example of 32B would be 3+2+2 (because *B* = 2) = 7 House Number

Here is the letter-and-numbers chart once again, for your convenience.

1	2	3	4	5	6	7	8	9
A	B	C	D	E	F	G	H	I
J	K	L	M	N	O	P	Q	R
S	T	U	V	W	X	Y	Z	

Let's now explore the House Number meanings.

1 House Number

A 1 House appeals to those who are independent and wish to stand on their own two feet. It's the ideal home for those who would like to be self-motivated, and accomplish their goals. This house will promote strength, courage, and individuality. If you like to live alone or prefer to work from home (especially as an independent contractor), a 1 House Number is the ideal number for you.

Challenge: Promotes competitiveness, aggressiveness, self-centeredness, or becoming overambitious.

2 House Number

A 2 House has a feminine energy and appeals to those who like nurturing and helping others. This house will promote partnership, sensitivity, and healing - therefore it's the ideal environment for a home-based healing business, or to enhance your psychic development. This house also encourages cooperation, compromise, and understanding of others.

Challenge: Amplifies the emotions and enhances jealousy, codependency, and giving too much of yourself to others.

3 House Number

A 3 House is ideal for artistic people looking to enhance their creative abilities. If you like to write, cook, decorate, design, paint, sing, dance, or create something using your imagination or your hands, this is the perfect house for you. If you're looking to raise children, entertain family and friends, or simply add a little more fun into your life, look no further than a 3 House.

Challenge: Encourages criticism, gossip, emotional highs and lows, and disorganization.

4 House Number

A 4 House Number is best suited to practical people who take their responsibilities seriously. This home promotes structure, order, and stability, so if you want to build a solid foundation for your future, this is the house for you. It is a good old-fashioned family home that will enable you to commit yourself to your goals.

Challenge: Inspires hard work and extra effort, so make time for fun and relaxation while living in this home.

5 House Number

A 5 House is an action-packed home with a lot going on. This home promotes activity, change, and adventure, so if you're a mover and shaker, this is the ideal home for you. Communication flows freely and it's a great place to socialize and entertain in. It's the ideal home for those who like to travel and get the most out of life.

Challenge: Encourages disorganization, unexpected events, overindulgence and extravagant behavior.

6 House Number

A 6 House is the ideal home in which to raise a family. Children, animals, and gardens thrive in the energy of a 6 home, as it feels comforting and inviting to all. This house inspires love, creativity, beauty, and friendship. It's the ideal home for a home-based beauty, childcare, cooking, clothing, counseling, or healing business.

Challenge: Promotes perfectionism, martyrdom and interference in others' lives.

7 House Number

A 7 House is ideal for those who like to relax and spend quiet time alone. If you're looking for a suitable environment in which to study and become a specialist in your craft, this is the house for you. This home promotes contemplation as well as personal and spiritual growth. It's the ideal home for healers and intuitive readers, analysts, scientists, technicians, teachers, and students.

Challenge: Provides a potentially challenging vibration for couples and families. Extra effort is required to stay connected to loved ones who reside within the home.

8 House Number

An 8 House is the ideal home for entrepreneurs and those who are dedicated to their careers. 8 promotes abundance and recognition, so if you understand the Law of Attraction, have a positive mind-set, live with honesty and integrity, and have a healthy relationship with money, this house can help you to manifest your dreams.

Challenge: Encourages manipulation, greed, big expenses, and financial loss.

9 House Number

A 9 House is ideal for those who wish to serve humanity, the community, or simply people in need. This home promotes healing, compassion, tolerance, and transformation. If you're creative and have a love of the arts or are a humanitarian at heart, this is the home for you. This house will encourage you to forgive and heal the past.

Challenge: Intensifies the emotions and encourages impatience and frustration.

Interesting fact

When evaluating a House Number look at each of the numbers individually prior to reducing down, because these have a minor influence, too. For example, in the number 4561 take a look at 4, 5, 6, and 1 before reducing down to 7.

Recurring Numbers

Do certain numbers follow you around? Do you keep seeing 11:11 everywhere and wonder what it means? Recurring numbers are the Universe's way of getting your attention when there is something important you need to know. You can think of recurring numbers as little messages from your guides, angels, and helpers to assist you on your path. In most cases, when these messages are acknowledged and followed, they can improve your quality of life.

Recurring numbers can present themselves in many different ways. They may appear as a sequence of numbers continually appearing on a clock, watch, computer screen, cell phone, license plate, or shopping receipt, or even in your dreams! Or you may come into contact with the same repetitive number in a variety of situations, such as sitting in the same seat number at the movies, always being allocated the same locker number at the gym, or always living in a house or apartment with the same number.

It isn't important how or where these numbers appear, it's the number (or sequence of numbers) themselves, that have the greatest meaning of all. Even though it may spook you at the time, it's important to follow up on what the numbers could mean because – let's face it – we could all do with a little assistance from above to help us on our path!

How to interpret the numbers

In numerology, each number has a variety of meanings, so there are several possibilities as to what the exact message of a number, or sequence of numbers, could be. This is where your intuition and common sense are required, because only through honest self-examination and evaluation can you possibly determine their meaning. Because a number has the same meaning wherever it appears, this applies to recurring numbers, too.

Number combinations

In the case of recurring number combinations – for example, 645 or 48 – the message will be a combination of each individual number's themes. For example, 645 could mean: love is on its way (6) once you create stability in your life (4) and make positive changes (5).

Recurring number meanings

Recurring 1's

- Create a new beginning/new beginnings are coming/ start something new
- Leave the past behind/be courageous and strong/be independent
- Break away from the pack/embrace your individuality

- Put your creative talents to good use/you create what you think – so watch your thoughts at all times
- Focus your attention on what you *want* rather than what you *don't want*
- Take action/be proactive.

Interesting fact: 11:11

11.11 is the most common recurring number sequence, witnessed by hundreds of thousands of people across the world. The presence of four number 1's (or two Master Number 11's) make it one of the most powerful number sequences ever – and its message is equally as powerful!

If you happen to see 11:11 at any time in your life, you are being asked to pay special attention to what you are thinking at that moment in time. Seeing 11:11 is a reminder that you are a powerful creative being and that your *thoughts attract things*. By focusing only on the things you want (as opposed to things you *don't* want) – you can attract them into your life.

Increased Awareness

Seeing 11:11 tells you to stop and be more aware. When this combination appears, ask yourself these questions:

- What am I thinking right now?
- What's going on in my life?
- Am I being positive and hopeful or am I angry, frustrated, worrying, obsessing or fearful?

When you see 11:11 you are being encouraged to raise your awareness of the energetic world around you, to look beyond what you see with your physical eyes and to tap into your inner knowing.

The combination 11:11 is telling you to follow your intuition, to raise your consciousness, and to call on the Universe (Source, God, the Divine) and your guides, angels, and helpers for assistance.

Recurring 2's

- Cooperate with others/be diplomatic/work on your relationships
- Heal your unresolved emotions/receive healing/heal others/love yourself
- Prepare for a romantic relationship that may be coming into your life
- Create balance in your life/learn to say no/be harmonious/begin a partnership
- Embrace your feminine side/follow your intuition/develop your psychic abilities

Recurring 3's

- Express yourself creatively/take up a new hobby/go on vacation
- Have more fun/spend more time with friends/be social
- Be honest and speak your truth/communicate with others/write or journal
- Express your emotions in a healthy way/put your feelings into words
- Be mindful of gossip, criticism, and complaining/be childlike

Recurring 4's

- Ground yourself/create more stability in your life/be disciplined
- Don't give up/work hard/save money/be honest/do the right thing
- Start building a foundation for your future/focus on your health/spend time in nature
- Know that the angels are around you/put your ideas into physical form

Recurring 5's

- Prepare for change/make positive changes/be flexible/go with the flow
- Break free from restraints/be adventurous/experience life/meet new people
- Be progressive/travel/go on vacation/exercise temperance and moderation
- Communicate your thoughts and ideas/promote yourself/take a risk

Recurring 6's

- Love is on its way/put effort into your relationships/spend quality time with your children
- Be there for your family and friends/work through family issues/be of service to others
- Love yourself/focus on your health/beautify your life and home/get a makeover

- Heal others/receive healing/take your responsibilities seriously
- Get married/start a family/prepare for a baby on the way

Recurring 7's

- Spend quiet time alone/pray regularly/take up yoga, qi gong, and/or meditation/focus on your health
- Discover the secrets and mysteries of the Universe/explore alternative therapies/study metaphysics
- Focus on your personal development/connect with Spirit/discover your spiritual truth
- Read/study or do research/go back to school/specialize in something/master your craft
- Teach others/travel/spend time in nature and the outdoors (especially in or near water)

Recurring 8's

- Budget your finances/deal with outstanding debts and legal matters/your finances will improve
- Focus on your career/change your job/consider self-employment
- Watch your thoughts at all times/be positive/adopt an attitude of abundance
- Balance the material and spiritual worlds/reclaim your personal power/rise above your ego
- Accept the recognition that is coming your way/be assured that justice will be served

Recurring 9's

- Prepare for endings and completion/be open to transformation/let go of what no longer serves you
- Trust and surrender/be tolerant/open your mind/forgive yourself and others/heal issues from the past
- Resolve outstanding conflicts/heal your relationships with family/be compassionate
- Give selflessly to others/follow humanitarian, animal-related, or environmental pursuits
- Express yourself creatively/explore the arts

Because the Law of Attraction enables you to attract what you focus your attention on, it is also possible to attract recurring numbers into your life simply by focusing your attention on them. With that being said, regardless of whether you attracted them or they were sent from the higher realms, recurring numbers can provide valuable guidance in your life.

Afterword

If you've made it to the end of this book, you deserve a giant pat on the back! Well done! Admittedly, numerology isn't for everyone. Some people find all of the numbers overwhelming and confusing, where others just "get it" and thrive on the challenge of working them out. If you're one of the fortunate ones who "gets it," then start preparing for a positive change because your life will never be the same.

Now that you have the ability to understand yourself and others better, and now that you have the blueprint for your life, you're one step ahead of the game - the game of life, that is! With an understanding of your numbers, you've awakened to a life of opportunity during which you can capitalize on your wisdom and play a better game. The gift of insight is priceless, and thanks to numerology, you have it in the palm of your hands!

You can use numerology for work or pleasure and you can calculate the charts for your colleagues, loved ones, and friends. Just be diplomatic and compassionate when relaying sensitive information such as life lessons, weaknesses, and challenges. It takes dedication, patience, and time to be an accurate and professional numerologist and until you reach that level, be responsible with this wisdom. Some people will believe everything you say, so be gentle in your approach and let them know you're still learning.

No method of forecasting and prediction can be 100 percent correct and while you're still learning you can avoid misinforming others (and yourself) by taking these with a pinch of salt. When you've developed an accurate understanding of the system, you can take it to a higher level where the opportunities are endless. In the meantime, with an understanding of your destiny and life purpose, you can begin to reach your full potential and make your dreams come true.

I wish you the very best on your journey. And from the bottom of my heart, I thank you for giving me the honor of teaching you numerology.

Love and blessings,

Michelle

Glossary

Birth Day Number: The "day" of a birth date; indicates personality traits, talents, and abilities that will assist you on your life path toward fulfilling your destiny.

Calendar Day Number: The number associated with the calendar day of the month.

Calendar Month Number: The number associated with the calendar month.

Calendar Year Number: The number associated with the calendar year.

Challenges/Challenge Numbers: Calculated from the month, day, and year of your birth date; identify four specific challenges that must be overcome in order for you to reach your full potential.

Current Name Number: Calculated from the first and last name used on a daily basis; offers additional traits, strengths, lessons, experiences, and opportunities to assist you on your journey.

Destiny Number: Calculated from the full original birth-certificate name; the second most significant number in your numerology chart; reveals your mission in this life, who and what you're destined to be.

First Challenge Number: Month of birth minus day of birth (or find the difference by subtracting the smaller number from the larger).

First Challenge Period: From birth (age 0) until the age of your Life Path Number subtracted from 36.

First Major Life Cycle Number: The number of your birth month; influences the first 25 to 35 years of your life.

First Major Life Cycle Period: A period calculated from your Life Path Number.

First Pinnacle Number: Month of birth plus day of birth.

First Pinnacle Period: From birth (age 0) until the age of your Life Path Number subtracted from 36.

Fourth Challenge Number: Month of birth minus year of birth (or find the difference by subtracting the smaller number from the larger).

Fourth Challenge Period: Starts where the third period ends and continues until the end of your life.

Fourth Pinnacle Number: Month of birth plus year of birth.

Fourth Pinnacle Period: Starts where the third period ends and continues until the end of your life.

House Number: Calculated by adding all of the digits in the house number together and then reducing them to a single-digit number; relates directly to the house and reveals what inhabitants can expect while living there.

Karmic Debt Numbers: 13/4, 14/5, 16/7, or 19/1; indicate particular lessons that failed to be learned in previous lives and must be mastered in this lifetime.

Karmic Lesson Numbers: Calculated from the missing numbers in a birth-certificate name; indicate weaknesses, along with the specific areas in need of growth that must be addressed in this life.

Life Path Number: Calculated from your birth date; the most significant number in your numerology chart; reveals the path you've chosen to walk in this life and the lessons you've chosen to master on your journey.

Major Life Cycles: Three blocks of time that highlight the three stages of growth throughout your life.

Major Life Cycle Number: Calculated from the month, day, and year of a birth date; the number associated with a particular Major Life Cycle.

Master Numbers: 11/2, 22/4, and 33/6; higher-octave vibrations of the lower base numbers, 2, 4, and 6; indicate great potential to attain self-mastery during the course of this life.

Maturity Number: Calculated by adding the Life Path Number and the Destiny Number together; reveals your future potential and the ultimate goal of your life from 45 yrs+.

Numerology: The ancient science of numbers, with each number contributing a unique vibration to the story of your life.

Numerology Chart/Profile: A complete chart/profile of your personality and forecasting numbers.

Personal Day Number: Calculated by adding the Personal Month Number and Calendar Day Number together; reveals the influence of the day.

Personal Month Number: Calculated by adding the Personal Year Number and Calendar Month Number together; reveals the influence of the month.

Personal Year Cycle: Commences at birth and progresses through nine-year cycles throughout your life; a nine-year cycle of personal growth in which each Personal Year Number has a unique theme regarding the types of lessons and experiences you'll encounter for that year.

Personal Year Number: Calculated by adding the month and day of your birth date to the Universal Year Number (calendar year); contains the lessons, opportunities, and experiences you'll encounter during the course of that year.

Personality Number: Calculated from the consonants in the birth-certificate name; represents the "outer you," or how others perceive you.

Personality Numbers/seven Personality Numbers: The seven numbers that have the most significance with respect to your personality, future potential, and life's journey: Life Path Number, Destiny Number, Soul Number, Personality

Number, Maturity Number, Birth Day Number, and Current Name Number.

Pinnacles: Reveal the opportunities and events you'll be faced with during each Pinnacle period, along with your potential areas for achievement.

Pinnacle Numbers: Calculated from the month, day, and year of a birth date.

Recurring Numbers: A number or sequence of numbers continually appearing in your day-to-day life, which are messages from the Universe and the angels.

Second Challenge Number: Day of birth minus year of birth (or find the difference by subtracting the smaller number from the larger).

Second Major Life Cycle Number: The number of your birth day.

Second Major Life Cycle Period: A period calculated from your Life Path Number.

Second Pinnacle Number: Day of birth plus year of birth.

Second Pinnacle Period: Nine years in duration; commences where the first period ends.

Soul Number: Calculated from the vowels in the birth-certificate name; reveals what motivates you, who your soul needs you to be to feel complete.

Third Challenge Number: The difference between the First and Second Challenge Numbers.

Third Challenge Period: Nine years in duration; commences where the second period ends.

Third Major Life Cycle Number: The number of your birth year.

Third Major Life Cycle Period: A period calculated from your Life Path Number.

Third Pinnacle Number: First Pinnacle Number plus Second Pinnacle Number.

Third Pinnacle Period: Nine years in duration also; commences where the second period ends.

Universal Day Number: Calculated by adding the Universal Month Number to the Calendar Day Number of enquiry; has the same meaning as the Personal Day Number, except it applies to the world rather than an individual.

Universal Month Number: Calculated by adding the Universal Year Number to the Calendar Month Number of enquiry; has the same meaning as the Personal Month Number, except it applies to the world rather than an individual.

Universal Year Number: The total of the current calendar year; has the same meaning as the Personal Year Number, except it applies to the world rather than an individual.

Resources

Recommended reading

Buchanan, Michelle. *The Numerology Guidebook: Discover Your Destiny and the Blueprint of Your Life*, Hay House, 2013

Decoz, J. Hans. *Numerology*, Perigee Books, 2001

Drayer, Ruth. *Numerology: The Power In Numbers*, Square One Publishers, 2002

Hay, Louise L. *Colors and Numbers*, Hay House, 2011

Jordan, Juno. *The Romance in Your Name*, De Vorss Publications, 1984

Millman, Dan. *The Life You Were Born to Live*, H.J. Kramer, 1993

Phillips, David A. *The Complete Book of Numerology*, Hay House, 2005

Templeton, Rosemary. *Numerology: Numbers and Their Influence*, Rockpool Publishing, 2007

Websites

See my website: www.michellebuchanan.co.nz for details of my personal readings, workshops, *The Numerology Guidebook*, the *Numerology Guidance Cards*, the *Numerology Guidance Cards App*, and for customized Numerology Personality Profiles and Forecast Reports.

Acknowledgments

First and foremost, I would like to acknowledge my publisher, Hay House, for giving me this wonderful opportunity to teach numerology to the world. I would also like to thank Amy Kiberd, Ingrid Court-Jones, Julie Oughton, and everybody at the Hay House UK office, for helping to bring this book together.

If it wasn't for the numerologist who gave me my very first reading back in 1991, this book might not exist. So I would like to acknowledge and thank her, whoever she is and wherever she may be in the world. I would also like to acknowledge the late Francie Williams of the North Shore School of Parapsychology, who helped develop my understanding of numerology even further in the 1990's.

Most of all, I'd like to thank my two beautiful children, Ben and Ava, who have put up with me tapping away at my computer, busily writing this book. Thank you for your patience and unconditional love. I couldn't have picked better children if I'd tried. Thank you, too, to my parents, Ray and Marilyn Wilson, for being the best parents in the world and for believing in me and my dream, despite my ongoing obstacles and challenges.

I would also like to acknowledge and thank every single person who has been involved in the creation, production, selling, promotion, transportation, and distribution of this book. You're an important link in the chain, and your input is greatly appreciated. If it wasn't for you, my book might not be on the Internet and in bookshops. Thank you!

Also a big thank you to you, the reader, for taking the time to read my book. I truly appreciate your time, attention, and support because without *you*, I wouldn't be able to do what I love!

And finally, thank you, Archangels Michael and Gabriel, my spirit guides, guardian angels, Nana Bradley, and other loved ones in spirit, for your love, guidance, and protection, and for getting me to this point. I am very blessed. Thank you all!

ABOUT THE AUTHOR

Michelle Buchanan has studied numerology for more than 27 years. She was formerly the spiritual counselor for *Woman's Day* magazine (New Zealand), as well as the resident numerologist for Television New Zealand's *Good Morning*.

Michelle provides personal readings, workshops, and seminars to people all over the world. She is also a talented singer/songwriter and dedicated mother of two, based in Auckland, New Zealand.

www.michellebuchanan.co.nz